Natural Language Processing with Python Quick Start Guide

Going from a Python developer to an effective Natural Language Processing Engineer

Nirant Kasliwal

BIRMINGHAM - MUMBAI

Natural Language Processing with Python Quick Start Guide

Copyright © 2018 Packt Publishing

All rights reserved. No part of this book may be reproduced, stored in a retrieval system, or transmitted in any form or by any means, without the prior written permission of the publisher, except in the case of brief quotations embedded in critical articles or reviews.

Every effort has been made in the preparation of this book to ensure the accuracy of the information presented. However, the information contained in this book is sold without warranty, either express or implied. Neither the author, nor Packt Publishing or its dealers and distributors, will be held liable for any damages caused or alleged to have been caused directly or indirectly by this book.

Packt Publishing has endeavored to provide trademark information about all of the companies and products mentioned in this book by the appropriate use of capitals. However, Packt Publishing cannot guarantee the accuracy of this information.

Commissioning Editor: Pravin Dhandre
Acquisition Editor: Siddharth Mandal
Content Development Editor: Roshan Kumar
Technical Editor: Jinesh Topiwala
Copy Editor: Safis Editng
Project Coordinator: Hardik Bhinde
Proofreader: Safis Editing
Indexer: Priyanka Dhadke
Graphics: Jason Monteiro
Production Coordinator: Deepika Naik

First published: November 2018

Production reference: 1301118

Published by Packt Publishing Ltd.
Livery Place
35 Livery Street
Birmingham
B3 2PB, UK.

ISBN 978-1-78913-038-6

www.packtpub.com

mapt.io

Mapt is an online digital library that gives you full access to over 5,000 books and videos, as well as industry leading tools to help you plan your personal development and advance your career. For more information, please visit our website.

Why subscribe?

- Spend less time learning and more time coding with practical eBooks and Videos from over 4,000 industry professionals

- Improve your learning with Skill Plans built especially for you

- Get a free eBook or video every month

- Mapt is fully searchable

- Copy and paste, print, and bookmark content

Packt.com

Did you know that Packt offers eBook versions of every book published, with PDF and ePub files available? You can upgrade to the eBook version at www.packt.com and as a print book customer, you are entitled to a discount on the eBook copy. Get in touch with us at customercare@packtpub.com for more details.

At www.packt.com, you can also read a collection of free technical articles, sign up for a range of free newsletters, and receive exclusive discounts and offers on Packt books and eBooks.

Contributors

About the author

Nirant Kasliwal maintains an awesome list of NLP natural language processing resources. GitHub's machine learning collection features this as the go-to guide. Nobel Laureate Dr. Paul Romer found his programming notes on Jupyter Notebooks helpful. Nirant won the first ever NLP Google Kaggle Kernel Award. At Soroco, image segmentation and intent categorization are the challenges he works with. His state-of-the-art language modeling results are available as Hindi2vec.

About the reviewer

Kiran Raj Samarthyam is a technical lead at Soroco, where he develops trustworthy automation systems for enterprises. At Soroco, Kiran has worked extensively on natural language processing, and has built complex and scalable virtual assistants for leading enterprises.

Before joining Soroco, Kiran pursued an MS from IIIT Hyderabad, specializing in high-performance computing under the guidance of Dr. Kishore Kothapalli, where he worked on various research problems to optimize algorithms for GPGPU/hybrid (CPU + GPU) architectures. Kiran has also published research papers at international conferences as part of his research.

Kiran likes to blog and is a big fan of animated movies.

> *I would like to thank Nirant Kasliwal for the trust and opportunity afforded to me to review this book. This book doesn't just introduce you to natural language processing, but is also packed with examples, best practices of Python, utilities, and coding. I would also like to extend my thanks to my family members (especially my wife) for their support and time. Last, but by no means least, I would like to thank the team at Packt (Siddharth Mandal and Hardik Bhinde), in particular for coordinating and helping me to complete the review on time.*

Packt is searching for authors like you

If you're interested in becoming an author for Packt, please visit `authors.packtpub.com` and apply today. We have worked with thousands of developers and tech professionals, just like you, to help them share their insight with the global tech community. You can make a general application, apply for a specific hot topic that we are recruiting an author for, or submit your own idea.

Table of Contents

Preface	1
Chapter 1: Getting Started with Text Classification	5
What is NLP?	6
Why learn about NLP?	6
You have a problem in mind	7
Technical achievement	7
Do something new	7
Is this book for you?	8
NLP workflow template	8
Understanding the problem	9
Understanding and preparing the data	9
Quick wins – proof of concept	9
Iterating and improving	10
Algorithms	10
Pre-processing	10
Evaluation and deployment	11
Evaluation	11
Deployment	11
Example – text classification workflow	12
Launchpad – programming environment setup	12
Text classification in 30 lines of code	13
Getting the data	13
Text to numbers	14
Machine learning	15
Summary	20
Chapter 2: Tidying your Text	21
Bread and butter – most common tasks	22
Loading the data	22
Exploring the loaded data	25
Tokenization	26
Intuitive – split by whitespace	26
The hack – splitting by word extraction	27
Introducing Regexes	27
spaCy for tokenization	29
How does the spaCy tokenizer work?	30
Sentence tokenization	31
Stop words removal and case change	31
Stemming and lemmatization	34
spaCy for lemmatization	34
-PRON-	36
Case-insensitive	36

Table of Contents

Conversion – meeting to meet — 36
spaCy compared with NLTK and CoreNLP — 36
Correcting spelling — 37
    FuzzyWuzzy — 37
    Jellyfish — 39
    Phonetic word similarity — 41
        What is a phonetic encoding? — 42
        Runtime complexity — 44
Cleaning a corpus with FlashText — 44
Summary — 47

Chapter 3: Leveraging Linguistics — 49
Linguistics and NLP — 49
    Getting started — 50
    Introducing textacy — 51
    Redacting names with named entity recognition — 51
        Entity types — 55
    Automatic question generation — 57
        Part-of-speech tagging — 57
        Creating a ruleset — 59
    Question and answer generation using dependency parsing — 61
        Visualizing the relationship — 62
        Introducing textacy — 64
        Leveling up – question and answer — 66
    Putting it together and the end — 68
Summary — 68

Chapter 4: Text Representations - Words to Numbers — 69
Vectorizing a specific dataset — 70
Word representations — 72
    How do we use pre-trained embeddings? — 73
    KeyedVectors API — 74
        What is missing in both word2vec and GloVe? — 76
    How do we handle Out Of Vocabulary words? — 77
        Getting the dataset — 77
    Training fastText embedddings — 79
    Training word2vec embeddings — 80
    fastText versus word2vec — 81
Document embedding — 81
    Understanding the doc2vec API — 84
        Negative sampling — 85
        Hierarchical softmax — 85
    Data exploration and model evaluation — 88
Summary — 90

Chapter 5: Modern Methods for Classification — 91
Machine learning for text — 92

Sentiment analysis as text classification	93
Simple classifiers	93
Optimizing simple classifiers	93
Ensemble methods	93
Getting the data	94
Reading data	95
Simple classifiers	96
Logistic regression	97
Removing stop words	98
Increasing ngram range	99
Multinomial Naive Bayes	99
Adding TF-IDF	99
Removing stop words	99
Changing fit prior to false	100
Support vector machines	100
Decision trees	101
Random forest classifier	102
Extra trees classifier	102
Optimizing our classifiers	103
Parameter tuning using RandomizedSearch	103
GridSearch	106
Ensembling models	107
Voting ensembles – Simple majority (aka hard voting)	107
Voting ensembles – soft voting	109
Weighted classifiers	109
Removing correlated classifiers	110
Summary	**111**

Chapter 6: Deep Learning for NLP — 113
What is deep learning? — 114
Differences between modern machine learning methods — 114
Understanding deep learning — 115
Puzzle pieces — 115
Model — 116
Loss function — 116
Optimizer — 117
Putting it all together – the training loop — 117
Kaggle – text categorization challenge — 118
Getting the data — 118
Exploring the data — 119
Multiple target dataset — 120
Why PyTorch? — 121
PyTorch and torchtext — 122
Data loaders with torchtext — 123
Conventions and style — 123
Knowing the field — 124
Exploring the dataset objects — 126
Iterators — 129
BucketIterator — 129

BatchWrapper	131
Training a text classifier	133
Initializing the model	134
Putting the pieces together again	135
Training loop	136
Prediction mode	138
Converting predictions into a pandas DataFrame	138
Summary	**139**
Chapter 7: Building your Own Chatbot	**141**
Why chatbots as a learning example?	**141**
Why build a chatbot?	142
Quick code means word vectors and heuristics	**142**
Figuring out the right user intent	144
Use case – food order bot	144
Classifying user intent	146
Bot responses	149
Better response personalization	150
Summary	**151**
Chapter 8: Web Deployments	**153**
Web deployments	**153**
Model persistence	154
Model loading and prediction	157
Flask for web deployments	158
Summary	**162**
Other Books You May Enjoy	**163**
Index	**167**

Preface

Natural language processing (**NLP**) is the use of machines to manipulate natural language. This book teaches you how to build NLP applications with code and relevant case studies using Python. This book will introduce you to the basic vocabulary and a suggested workflow for building NLP applications to help you get started with popular NLP tasks such as sentiment analysis, entity recognition, part of speech tagging, stemming, and word embeddings.

Who this book is for

This book is for programmers who wish to build systems that can interpret language and who have exposure to Python programming. A familiarity with NLP vocabulary and basics and machine learning would be helpful, but is not mandatory.

What this book covers

Chapter 1, *Getting Started with Text Classification*, introduces the reader to NLP and what a good NLP workflow looks like. You will also learn how to prepare text for machine learning with scikit-learn.

Chapter 2, *Tidying Your Text*, discusses some of the most common text pre-processing ideas. You will be introduced to spaCy and will learn how to use it for tokenization, sentence extraction, and lemmatization.

Chapter 3, *Leveraging Linguistics*, goes into a simple use case and examines how we can solve it. Then, we repeat this task again, but on a slightly different text corpus.

Chapter 4, *Text Representations – Words to Numbers*, introduces readers to the Gensim API. We will also learn to load pre-trained GloVe vectors and to use these vector representations instead of TD-IDF in any machine learning model.

Chapter 5, *Modern Methods for Classification*, looks at several new ideas regarding machine learning. The intention here is to demonstrate some of the most common classifiers. We will also learn about concepts such as sentiment analysis, simple classifiers, and how to optimize them for your datasets and ensemble methods.

Preface

Chapter 6, *Deep Learning for NLP*, cover what deep learning is, how it differs from what we have seen, and the key ideas in any deep learning model. We will also look at a few topics regarding PyTorch, how to tokenize text, and what recurrent networks are.

Chapter 7, *Building Your Own Chatbot*, explains why chatbots should be built and figures out the correct user intent. We will also learn in detail about *intent* , *response*, *templates*, and *entities*.

Chapter 8, *Web Deployments*, explains how to train a model and write some neater utils for data I/O. We are going to build a predict function and expose it using a Flask REST endpoint.

To get the most out of this book

- You will need conda with Python 3.6 or new version
- A basic understanding to Python programming language will be required
- NLP or machine learning experience will be helpful but is not mandatory

Download the example code files

You can download the example code files for this book from your account at www.packt.com. If you purchased this book elsewhere, you can visit www.packt.com/support and register to have the files emailed directly to you.

You can download the code files by following these steps:

1. Log in or register at www.packt.com.
2. Select the **SUPPORT** tab.
3. Click on **Code Downloads & Errata**.
4. Enter the name of the book in the **Search** box and follow the onscreen instructions.

Once the file is downloaded, please make sure that you unzip or extract the folder using the latest version of:

- WinRAR/7-Zip for Windows
- Zipeg/iZip/UnRarX for Mac
- 7-Zip/PeaZip for Linux

The code bundle for the book is also hosted on GitHub at `https://github.com/PacktPublishing/Natural-Language-Processing-with-Python-Quick-Start-Guide`. In case there's an update to the code, it will be updated on the existing GitHub repository.

We also have other code bundles from our rich catalog of books and videos available at `https://github.com/PacktPublishing/`. Check them out!

Download the color images

We also provide a PDF file that has color images of the screenshots/diagrams used in this book. You can download it here: `http://www.packtpub.com/sites/default/files/downloads/9781789130386_ColorImages.pdf`.

Conventions used

There are a number of text conventions used throughout this book.

`CodeInText`: Indicates code words in text, database table names, folder names, filenames, file extensions, pathnames, dummy URLs, user input, and Twitter handles. Here is an example: "I used the `sed` syntax."

A block of code is set as follows:

```
url = 'http://www.gutenberg.org/ebooks/1661.txt.utf-8'
file_name = 'sherlock.txt'
```

Any command-line input or output is written as follows:

```
import pandas as pd
import numpy as np
```

Bold: Indicates a new term, an important word, or words that you see onscreen. For example, words in menus or dialog boxes appear in the text like this. Here is an example: "The **Prediction: pos** is actually a result from the file I uploaded to this page earlier."

 Warnings or important notes appear like this.

 Tips and tricks appear like this.

Get in touch

Feedback from our readers is always welcome.

General feedback: If you have questions about any aspect of this book, mention the book title in the subject of your message and email us at `customercare@packtpub.com`.

Errata: Although we have taken every care to ensure the accuracy of our content, mistakes do happen. If you have found a mistake in this book, we would be grateful if you would report this to us. Please visit `www.packt.com/submit-errata`, selecting your book, clicking on the Errata Submission Form link, and entering the details.

Piracy: If you come across any illegal copies of our works in any form on the internet, we would be grateful if you would provide us with the location address or website name. Please contact us at `copyright@packt.com` with a link to the material.

If you are interested in becoming an author: If there is a topic that you have expertise in, and you are interested in either writing or contributing to a book, please visit `authors.packtpub.com`.

Reviews

Please leave a review. Once you have read and used this book, why not leave a review on the site that you purchased it from? Potential readers can then see and use your unbiased opinion to make purchase decisions, we at Packt can understand what you think about our products, and our authors can see your feedback on their book. Thank you!

For more information about Packt, please visit `packt.com`.

1 Getting Started with Text Classification

There are several ways that you can learn new ideas and learn new skills. In an art class students study colors, but aren't allowed to actually paint until college. Sound absurd?

Unfortunately, this is how most modern machine learning is taught. The experts are doing something similar. They tell you that need to know linear algebra, calculus and deep learning. This is before they'll teach you how to use **natural language Processing** (**NLP**).

In this book, I want us to learn by teaching the the whole game. In every section, we see how to solve real-world problems and learn the tools along the way. Then, we will dig deeper and deeper into understanding how to make these toolks. This learning and teaching style is very much inspired by Jeremy Howard of fast.ai fame.

The next focus is to have code examples wherever possible. This is to ensure that there is a clear and motivating purpose behind learning a topic. This helps us understand with intuition, beyond math formulae with algebraic notation.

In this opening chapter, we will focus on an introduction to NLP. And, then jump into a text classification example with code.

This is what our journey will briefly look like:

- What is NLP?
- What does a good NLP workflow look like? This is to improve your success rate when working on any NLP project.
- Text classification as a motivating example for a good NLP pipeline/workflow.

What is NLP?

Natural language processing is the use of machines to manipulate natural language. In this book, we will focus on written language, or in simpler words: text.

In effect, this is a practitioner's guide to text processing in English.

Humans are the only known species to have developed written languages. Yet, children don't learn to read and write on their own. This is to highlight the complexity of text processing and NLP.

The study of natural language processing has been around for more than 50 years. The famous Turing test for general artificial intelligence uses this language. This field has grown both in regard to linguistics and its computational techniques.

In the spirit of being able to build things first, we will learn how to build a simple text classification system using Python's scikit-learn and no other dependencies.

We will also address if this book is a good pick for you.

Let's get going!

Why learn about NLP?

The best way to get the most about of this book is by knowing what you want NLP to do for you.

A variety of reasons might draw you to NLP. It might be the higher earning potential. Maybe you've noticed and are excited by the potential of NLP, for example, regarding Uber's customer Service bots. Yes, they mostly use bots to answer your complaints instead of humans.

It is useful to know your motivation and write it down. This will help you select problems and projects that excite you. It will also help you be selective when reading this book. This is not an NLP Made Easy or similar book. Let's be honest: this is a challenging topic. Writing down your motivations is a helpful reminder.

As a legal note, the accompanying code has a permissive MIT License. You can use it at your work without legal hassle. That being said, each dependent library is from a third party, and you should **definitely check** if they **allow commercial use or not.**

I don't expect you to be able to use all of the tools and techniques mentioned here. Cherry-pick things that make sense.

You have a problem in mind

You already have a problem in mind, such as an academic project or a problem at your work.

Are you looking for the best tools and techniques that you could use to get off the ground?

First, flip through to the book's index to check if I have covered your problem here. I have shared end-to-end solutions for some of the most common use cases here. If it is not shared, fret not—you are still covered. The underlying techniques for a lot of tasks are common. I have been careful to select methods that are useful to a wider audience.

Technical achievement

Is learning a mark of achievement for you?

NLP and, more generally, data science, are popular terms. You are someone who wants to keep up. You are someone who takes joy from learning new tools, techniques, and technologies. This is your next big challenge. This is your chance to prove your ability to self-teach and meet mastery.

If this sounds like you, you may be interested in using this as a reference book. I have dedicated sections where we give you enough understanding of a method. I show you how to use it without having to dive down into the latest papers. This is an invitation to learning more, and you are not encouraged to stop here. Try these code samples out for yourself!

Do something new

You have some domain expertise. Now, you want to do things in your domain that are not possible without these skills. One way to figure out new possibilities is to combine your domain expertise with what you learn here. There are several very large opportunities that I saw as I wrote this book, including the following:

- NLP for non-English languages such as Hindi, Tamil, or Telugu.
- Specialized NLP for your domain, for example, finance and Bollywood have different languages in their own ways. Your models that have been trained on Bollywood news are not expected to work for finance.

If this sounds like you, you want to pay attention to the text pre-processing sections in this book. These sections will help you understand how we make text ready for machine consumption.

Is this book for you?

This book has been written so that it keeps the preceding use cases and mindsets in mind. The methods, technologies, tools, and techniques selected here are a fine balance of industry-grade stability and academia-grade results quality. There are several tools, such as parfit, and Flashtext, and ideas such as LIME, that have never been written about in the context of NLP.

Lastly, I understand the importance and excitement of deep learning methods and have a dedicated chapter on deep learning for NLP methods.

NLP workflow template

Some of us would love to work on Natural Language Processing for its sheer intellectual challenges – across research and engineering. To measure our progress, having a workflow with rough time estimates is really valuable. In this short section, we will briefly outline what a usual NLP or even most applied machine learning processes look like.

Most people I've learned from like to use a (roughly) five-step process:

- Understanding the problem
- Understanding and preparing data
- Quick wins: proof of concepts
- Iterating and improving the results
- Evaluation and deployment

This is just a process template. It has a lot of room for customization regarding the engineering culture in your company. Any of these steps can be broken down further. For instance, data preparation and understanding can be split further into analysis and cleaning. Similarly, the proof of concept step may involve multiple experiments, and a demo or a report submission of best results from those.

Although this appears to be a strictly linear process, it is not so. More often than not, you will want to revisit a previous step and change a parameter or a particular data transform to see the effect on later performance.

In order to do so, it is important to factor in the cyclic nature of this process in your code. **Write code with well-designed abstractions with each component being independently reusable.**

 If you are interested in how to write better NLP code, especially for research or experimentation, consider looking up the slide deck titled *Writing Code for NLP Research*, by Joel Grus of AllenAI.

Let's expand a little bit into each of these sections.

Understanding the problem

We will begin by understanding the requirements and constraints from a practical business view point. This tends to answer the following the questions:

- What is the main problem? We will try to understand – formally and informally – the assumptions and expectations from our project.
- How will I solve this problem? List some ideas that you might have seen earlier or in this book. This is the list that you will use to plan your work ahead.

Understanding and preparing the data

Text and language is inherently unstructured. We might want to clean it in certain ways, such as expanding abbreviations and acronyms, removing punctuation, and so on. We also want to select a few samples that are the best representatives of the data we might see in the wild.

The other common practice is to prepare a gold dataset. A gold dataset is the best available data under reasonable conditions. This is not the best available data under ideal conditions. Creating the gold dataset often involves manual tagging and cleaning processes.

The next few sections are dedicated to text cleaning and text representations at this stage of the NLP workflow.

Quick wins – proof of concept

We want to quickly spot the types of algorithms and dataset combinations that sort of work for us. We can then focus on them and study them in greater detail.

The results from here will help you estimate the amount of work ahead of you. For instance, if you are going to develop a search system for documents based exclusively on keywords, your main effort will probably be deploying an open source solution such as ElasticSearch.

Let's say that you now want to add a similar documents feature. Depending on the expected quality of results, you will want to look into techniques such as doc2vec and word2vec, or even some convolutional neural network solution using Keras/Tensorflow or PyTorch.

This step is essential to get a greater buy-in from others around you, such as your boss, to invest more energy and resources into this. In an engineering role, this demo should highlight parts of your work that the shelf systems usually can't do. These are your unique strengths. These are usually insights, customization, and control that other systems can't provide.

Iterating and improving

At this point, we have a selected list of algorithms, data, and methods that have encouraging results for us.

Algorithms

If your algorithms are machine learning or statistical in nature, you will quite often have a lot of juice left.

There are quite often parameters for which you simply pick a good enough default during the earlier stage. Here, you might want to double down and check for the best value of those parameters. This idea is sometimes referred to as parameter search, or hyperparameter tuning in machine learning parlance.

You might want to combine the results of one technique with the other in particular ways. For instance, some statistical methods might be very good for finding noun phrases in your text and using them to classify it, while a deep learning method (let's call it DL-LSTM) might be the best suited for text classification of the entire document. In that case, you might want to pass the extra information from both your noun phrase extraction and DL-LSTM to another model. This will allow it to the use the best of both worlds. This idea is sometimes referred to as stacking in machine learning parlance. This was quite successful on the machine learning contest platform Kaggle until very recently.

Pre-processing

Simple changes in data pre-processing or the data cleaning stage can quite often give you dramatically better results. For instance, making sure that your entire corpus is in lowercase can help you reduce the number of unique words (your vocabulary size) by a significant fraction.

 If your numeric representation of words is skewed by the word frequency, sometimes it helps to normalize and/or scale the same. The laziest hack is to simply divide by the frequency.

Evaluation and deployment

Evaluation and deployment are critical components in making your work widely available. The quality of your evaluation determines how trustworthy your work is by other people. Deployment varies widely, but quite often is abstracted out in single function calls or REST API calls.

Evaluation

Let's say you have a model with 99% accuracy in classifying brain tumors. Can you trust this model? No.

If your model had said that no-one has a brain tumor, it would still have 99%+ accuracy. Why?

Because luckily 99% or more of the population does not have a brain tumor!

To use our models for practical use, we need to look beyond accuracy. We need to understand what the model gets right or wrong in order to improve it. A minute spent understanding the confusion matrix will stop us from going ahead with such dangerous models.

Additionally, we will want to develop an intuition of what the model is doing underneath the black box optimization algorithms. Data visualization techniques such as t-SNE can assist us with this.

For continuously running NLP applications such as email spam classifiers or chatbots, we would want the evaluation of the model quality to happen continuously as well. This will help us ensure that the model's performance does not degrade with time.

Deployment

This book is written with a programmer-first mindset. We will learn how to deploy any machine learning or NLP application as a REST API which can then be used for the web and mobile. This architecture is quite prevalent in the industry. For instance, we know that this is how data science teams such as those at Amazon and LinkedIn deploy their work to the web.

Example – text classification workflow

The preceding process is fairly generic. What would it look like for one of the most common natural language applications – text classification?

The following flow diagram was built by Microsoft Azure, and is used here to explain how their own technology fits directly into our workflow template. There are several new words that they have introduced to feature engineering, such as unigrams, TF-IDF, TF, n-grams, and so on:

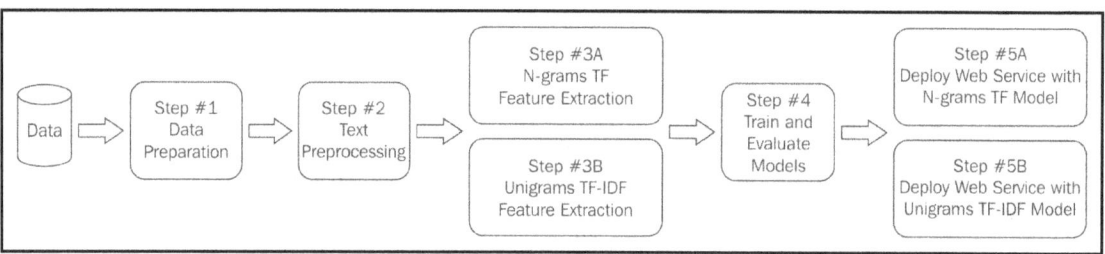

The main steps in their flow diagram are as follows:

1. **Step 1**: Data preparation
2. **Step 2**: Text pre-processing
3. **Step 3**: Feature engineering:
    - Unigrams TF-IDF extraction
    - N-grams TF extraction
4. **Step 4**: Train and evaluate models
5. **Step 5**: Deploy trained models as web services

This means that it's time to stop talking and start programming. Let's quickly set up the environment first and then we will work on building our first text classification system in 30 lines of code or less.

Launchpad – programming environment setup

We will use the fast.ai machine learning setup for this exercise. Their setup environment is great for personal experimentation and industry-grade proof-of-concept projects. I have used the fast.ai environment on both Linux and Windows. We will use Python 3.6 here since our code will not run for other Python versions.

A quick search on their forums will also take you to the latest instructions on how to set up the same on most cloud computing solutions including AWS, Google Cloud Platform, and Paperspace.

This environment covers the tools that we will use across most of the major tasks that we will perform: text processing (including cleaning), feature extraction, machine learning and deep learning models, model evaluation, and deployment.

It includes spaCy out of the box. spaCy is an open source tool that was made for an industry-grade NLP toolkit. If someone recommends that you use NLTK for a task, use spaCy instead. The demo ahead works out of the box in their environment.

There are a few more packages that we will need for later tasks. We will install and set them up as and when required. We don't want to bloat your installation with unnecessary packages that you might not even use.

Text classification in 30 lines of code

Let's divide the classification problem into the following steps:

1. Getting the data
2. Text to numbers
3. Running ML algorithms with sklearn

Getting the data

The 20 newsgroups dataset is a fairly well-known dataset among the NLP community. It is near-ideal for demonstration purposes. This dataset has a near-uniform distribution across 20 classes. This uniform distribution makes iterating rapidly on classification and clustering techniques easy.

We will use the famous 20 newsgroups dataset for our demonstrations as well:

```
from sklearn.datasets import fetch_20newsgroups   # import packages which
help us download dataset
twenty_train = fetch_20newsgroups(subset='train', shuffle=True,
download_if_missing=True)
twenty_test = fetch_20newsgroups(subset='test', shuffle=True,
download_if_missing=True)
```

Getting Started with Text Classification

Most modern NLP methods rely heavily on machine learning methods. These methods need words that are written as strings of text to be converted into a numerical representation. This numerical representation can be as simple as assigning a unique integer ID to slightly more comprehensive vector of float values. In the case of the latter, this is sometimes referred to as vectorization.

Text to numbers

We will be using a bag of words model for our example. We simply convert the number of times every word occurs per document. Therefore, each document is a bag and we count the frequency of each word in that bag. This also means that we lose any *ordering* information that's present in the text. Next, we assign each unique word an integer ID. All of these unique words become our vocabulary. Each word in our vocabulary is treated as a machine learning feature. Let's make our vocabulary first.

Scikit-learn has a high-level component that will create feature vectors for us. This is called `CountVectorizer`. We recommend reading more about it from the scikit-learn docs:

```
# Extracting features from text files
from sklearn.feature_extraction.text import CountVectorizer

count_vect = CountVectorizer()
X_train_counts = count_vect.fit_transform(twenty_train.data)

print(f'Shape of Term Frequency Matrix: {X_train_counts.shape}')
```

By using `count_vect.fit_transform(twenty_train.data)`, we are learning the vocabulary dictionary, which returns a Document-Term matrix of shape [n_samples, n_features]. This means that we have n_samples documents or bags with n_features unique words across them.

We will now be able to extract a meaningful relationship between these words and the tags or classes they belong to. One of the simplest ways to do this is to count the number of times a word occurs in each class.

We have a small issue with this – long documents then tend to influence the result a lot more. We can normalize this effect by dividing the word frequency by the total words in that document. We call this Term Frequency, or simply TF.

Words like *the*, *a*, and *of* are common across all documents and don't really help us distinguish between document classes or separate them. We want to emphasize rarer words, such as *Manmohan* and *Modi*, over common words. One way to do this is to use inverse document frequency, or IDF. Inverse document frequency is a measure of whether the term is common or rare in all documents.

We multiply TF with IDF to get our TF-IDF metric, which is always greater than zero. TF-IDF is calculated for a triplet of term t, document d, and vocab dictionary D.

We can directly calculate TF-IDF using the following lines of code:

```
from sklearn.feature_extraction.text import TfidfTransformer

tfidf_transformer = TfidfTransformer()
X_train_tfidf = tfidf_transformer.fit_transform(X_train_counts)

print(f'Shape of TFIDF Matrix: {X_train_tfidf.shape}')
```

The last line will output the dimension of the Document-Term matrix, which is (11314, 130107).

Please note that in the preceding example we used each word as a feature, so the TF-IDF was calculated for each word. When we use a single word as a feature, we call it a unigram. If we were to use two consecutive words as a feature instead, we'd call it a bigram. In general, for n-words, we would call it an n-gram.

Machine learning

Various algorithms can be used for text classification. You can build a classifier in scikit using the following code:

```
from sklearn.linear_model import LogisticRegression as LR
from sklearn.pipeline import Pipeline
```

Let's dissect the preceding code, line by line.

The initial two lines are simple imports. We import the fairly well-known Logistic Regression model and rename the import LR. The next is a pipeline import:

> "Sequentially apply a list of transforms and a final estimator. Intermediate steps of the pipeline must be "transforms", that is, they must implement fit and transform methods. The final estimator only needs to implement fit."
>
> *- from* `sklearn docs`

Getting Started with Text Classification

Scikit-learn pipelines are, logistically, lists of operations that are applied, one after another. First, we applied the two operations we have already seen: `CountVectorizer()` and `TfidfTransformer()`. This was followed by `LR()`. The pipeline was created with `Pipeline(...)`, but hasn't been executed. It is only executed when we call the `fit()` function from the `Pipeline` object:

```
text_lr_clf = Pipeline([('vect', CountVectorizer()), ('tfidf', 
TfidfTransformer()), ('clf',LR())])
text_lr_clf = text_lr_clf.fit(twenty_train.data, twenty_train.target)
```

When this is called, it calls the transform function of all but the last object. For the last object – our Logistic Regression classifier – its `fit()` function is called. These transforms and classifiers are also referred to as estimators:

> *"All estimators in a pipeline, except the last one, must be transformers (that is, they must have a transform method). The last estimator may be any type (transformer, classifier, and so on)."*
>
> *- from* `sklearn pipeline docs`

Let's calculate the accuracy of this model on the test data. For calculating the means on a large number of values, we will be using a scientific library called `numpy`:

```
import numpy as np
lr_predicted = text_lr_clf.predict(twenty_test.data)
lr_clf_accuracy = np.mean(lr_predicted == twenty_test.target) * 100.

print(f'Test Accuracy is {lr_clf_accuracy}')
```

This prints out the following output:

```
Test Accuracy is 82.79341476367499
```

We used the LR default parameters here. We can later optimize these using `GridSearch` or `RandomSearch` to improve the accuracy even more.

 If you're going to remember only one thing from this section, remember to try a linear model such as logistic regression. They are often quite good for sparse high-dimensional data such as text, bag-of-words, or TF-IDF.

Chapter 1

In addition to accuracy, it is useful to understand which categories of text are being confused for which other categories. We will call this a confusion matrix.

The following code uses the same variables we used to calculate the test accuracy for finding out the confusion matrix:

```
from sklearn.metrics import confusion_matrix
cf = confusion_matrix(y_true=twenty_test.target, y_pred=lr_predicted)
print(cf)
```

This prints a giant list of numbers which is not very interpretable. Let's try pretty printing this by using the print-json hack:

```
import json
print(json.dumps(cf.tolist(), indent=2))
```

This returns the following code:

```
[
  [
    236,
    2,
    0,
    0,
    1,
    1,
    3,
    0,
    3,
    3,
    1,
    1,
    2,
    9,
    2,
    35,
    3,
    4,
    1,
    12
  ],
  ...
  [
    38,
    4,
    0,
    0,
    0,
```

[17]

```
            0,
            4,
            0,
            0,
            2,
            2,
            0,
            0,
            8,
            3,
           48,
           17,
            2,
            9,
          114
        ]
    ]
```

This is slightly better. We now understand that this is a 20 × 20 grid of numbers. However, interpreting these numbers is a tedious task unless we can bring some visualization into this game. Let's do that next:

```
# this line ensures that the plot is rendered inside the Jupyter we used
for testing this code
%matplotlib inline

import seaborn as sns
import matplotlib.pyplot as plt

plt.figure(figsize=(20,10))
ax = sns.heatmap(cf, annot=True, fmt="d",linewidths=.5, center = 90, vmax = 200)
# plt.show() # optional, un-comment if the plot does not show
```

This gives us the following amazing plot:

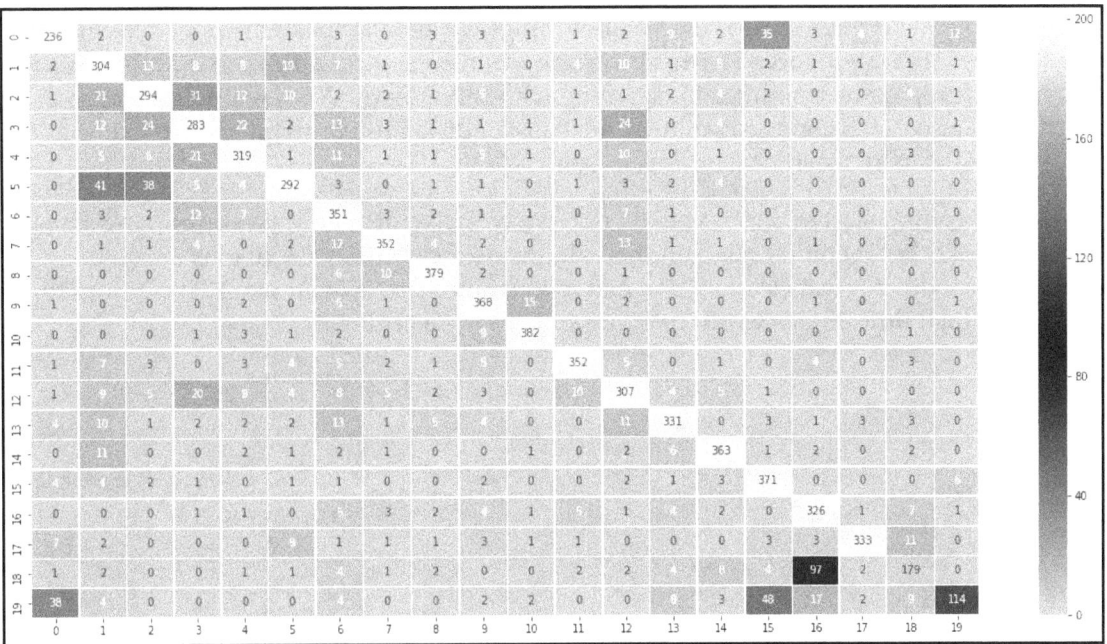

This plot highlights information of interest to us in different color schemes. For instance, the light diagonal from the lupper-left corner to the lower-right corner shows everything we got right. The other grids are darker-colored if we confused those more. For instance, 97 samples of one class got wrongly tagged, which is quickly visible by the dark black color in row **18** and column **16**.

We will dive deeper into both parts of this section – model interpretation and data visualization – in slightly more detail later in this book.

Summary

In this chapter, you got a feel for the broader things we need to make the project work. We saw the steps that are involved in this process by using a text classification example. We saw how to prepare text for machine learning with scikit-learn. We saw Logistic Regression for ML. We also saw a confusion matrix, which is a quick and powerful tool for making sense of results in all machine learning, beyond NLP.

We are just getting started. From here on out, we will dive deeper into each of these steps and see what other methods exist out there. In the next chapter, we will look at some common methods for text cleaning and extraction. Since this is what we will spend up to 80% of our total time on, it's worth the time and energy learning it.

2
Tidying your Text

Data cleaning is one of the most important and time-consuming tasks when it comes to **natural language processing** (**NLP**):

> *"There's the joke that 80 percent of data science is cleaning the data and 20 percent is complaining about cleaning the data."*
>
> – *Kaggle founder and CEO Anthony Goldbloom in a* `Verge Interview`

In this chapter, we will discuss some of the most common text pre-processing ideas. This task is universal, tedious, and unavoidable. Most people working in data science or NLP understand that it's an underrated value addition. Some of these tasks don't work well in isolation but have a powerful effect when used in the right combination and order. This chapter will introduce several new words and tools, since the field has a rich history from two worlds. It borrows from both traditional NLP and machine learning. We'll meet spaCy, a fast industry-grade toolkit for natural language processing in Python. We will use it for tokenization, sentence extraction, and lemmatization.

We will learn to use regex functions, which are useful for text mining. Python's regex replaces can be slow for larger data sizes. Instead, we will use FlashText for substitution and expansion.

This is the only book to cover FlashText. More broadly, we will share how you can start thinking about manipulating and cleaning text. This is not an in-depth coverage of any one technique, but a jump start for you to think about what might work for you.

Bread and butter – most common tasks

There are several well-known text cleaning ideas. They have all made their way into the most popular tools today such as NLTK, Stanford CoreNLP, and spaCy. I like spaCy for two main reasons:

- It's an industry-grade NLP, unlike NLTK, which is mainly meant for teaching.
- It has good speed-to-performance trade-off. spaCy is written in Cython, which gives it C-like performance with Python code.

spaCy is actively maintained and developed, and incorporates the best methods available for most challenges.

By the end of this section, you will be able to do the following:

- Understand tokenization and do it manually yourself using spaCy
- Understand why stop word removal and case standardization works, with spaCy examples
- Differentiate between stemming and lemmatization, with spaCy lemmatization examples

Loading the data

I have always liked *The Adventures of Sherlock Holmes* by Sir Arthur Conan Doyle. Let's download the book and save it locally:

```
url = 'http://www.gutenberg.org/ebooks/1661.txt.utf-8'
file_name = 'sherlock.txt'
```

Let's actually download the file. You only need to do this once, but this download utility can be used whenever you are downloading other datasets, too:

```
import urllib.request
# Download the file from `url` and save it locally under `file_name`:
with urllib.request.urlopen(url) as response:
    with open(file_name, 'wb') as out_file:
        data = response.read() # a `bytes` object
        out_file.write(data)
```

Moving on, let's check whether we got the correct file in place with shell syntax inside our Jupyter notebook. This ability to run basic shell commands – on both Windows and Linux – is really useful:

```
!ls *.txt
```

The preceding command returns the following output:

```
sherlock.txt
```

The file contains header and footer information from Project Gutenberg. We are not interested in this, and will discard the copyright and other legal notices. This is what we want to do:

1. Open the file.
2. Delete the header and footer information.
3. Save the new file as `sherlock_clean.txt`.

I opened the text file and found that I need to remove the first 33 lines. Let's do that using shell commands – which also work on Windows inside Jupyter notebook. You remember this now, don't you? Marching on:

```
!sed -i 1,33d sherlock.txt
```

I used the `sed` syntax. The `-i` flag tells you to make the necessary changes. `1,33d` instructs you to delete lines 1 to 33.

Let's double-check this. We expect the book to now begin with the iconic book title/cover:

```
!head -5 sherlock.txt
```

This shows the first five lines of the book. They are as we expect:

```
THE ADVENTURES OF SHERLOCK HOLMES

    by

    SIR ARTHUR CONAN DOYLE
```

Tidying your Text

What do I see?

Before I move on to text cleaning for any NLP task, I would like to spend a few seconds taking a quick glance at the data itself. I noted down some of the things I spotted in the following list. Of course, a keener eye will be able to see a lot more than I did:

- Dates are written in a mixed format: *twentieth of March, 1888*; times are too: *three o'clock*.
- The text is wrapped at around 70 columns, so no line can be longer than 70 characters.
- There are a lot of proper nouns. These include names such as *Atkinson* and *Trepoff*, in addition to locations such as *Trincomalee* and *Baker Street*.
- The index is in Roman numerals such as *I* and *IV*, and not *1* and *4*.
- There is a lot of dialogues such as *You have carte blanche,* with no narrative around them. This storytelling style switches freely from being narrative to dialogue-driven.
- The grammar and vocabulary is slightly unusual because of the time when Doyle wrote.

These subjective observations are helpful in understanding the nature and edge cases in your text. Let's move on and load the book into Python for processing:

```
# let's get this data into Python

text = open(file_name, 'r', encoding='utf-8').read() # note that I add an encoding='utf-8' parameter to preserve information

print(text[:5])
```

This returns the first five characters:

```
THE A
```

Let's quickly verify that we have loaded the data into useful data types.

To check our own data types, use the following command:

```
print(f'The file is loaded as datatype: {type(text)} and has {len(text)} characters in it')
```

The preceding command returns the following output:

```
The file is loaded as datatype: <class 'str'> and has 581204 characters in it
```

There is a major improvement between Py2.7 and Py3.6 on how strings are handled. They are now all Unicode by default.

In Python 3, `str` are Unicode strings, and it is more convenient for the NLP of non-English texts.

Here is a small relevant example to highlight the differences between the two:

```
from collections import Counter
Counter('Möbelstück')

In Python 2: Counter({'\xc3': 2, 'b': 1, 'e': 1, 'c': 1, 'k': 1, 'M': 1,
'l': 1, 's': 1, 't': 1, '\xb6': 1, '\xbc': 1})
In Python 3: Counter({'M': 1, 'ö': 1, 'b': 1, 'e': 1, 'l': 1, 's': 1, 't':
1, 'ü': 1, 'c': 1, 'k': 1})
```

Exploring the loaded data

How many unique characters can we see?

For reference, ASCII has 127 characters in it, so we expect this to have, at most, 127 characters:

```
unique_chars = list(set(text))
unique_chars.sort()
print(unique_chars)
print(f'There are {len(unique_chars)} unique characters, including both
ASCII and Unicode character')
```

The preceding code returns the following output:

```
    ['\n', ' ', '!', '"', '$', '%', '&', "'", '(', ')', '*', ',', '-', '.',
'/', '0', '1', '2', '3', '4', '5', '6', '7', '8', '9', ':', ';', '?', '@',
'A', 'B', 'C', 'D', 'E', 'F', 'G', 'H', 'I', 'J', 'K', 'L', 'M', 'N', 'O',
'P', 'Q', 'R', 'S', 'T', 'U', 'V', 'W', 'X', 'Y', 'Z', 'a', 'b', 'c', 'd',
'e', 'f', 'g', 'h', 'i', 'j', 'k', 'l', 'm', 'n', 'o', 'p', 'q', 'r', 's',
't', 'u', 'v', 'w', 'x', 'y', 'z', 'à', 'â', 'è', 'é']
    There are 85 unique characters, including both ASCII and Unicode
character
```

For our machine learning models, we often need the words to occur as individual tokens or single words. Let's explain what this means in the next section.

Tokenization

Given a character sequence and a defined document unit, tokenization is the task of chopping it up into pieces, called tokens , perhaps at the same time throwing away certain characters, such as punctuation.
Here is an example of tokenization:

```
Input: Friends, Romans, Countrymen, lend me your ears;
Output: Friends  Romans  Countrymen  lend  me  your  ears .
```

It is, in fact, sometimes useful to distinguish between tokens and words. But here, for ease of understanding, we will use them interchangeably.

We will convert the raw text into a list of words. This should preserve the original ordering of the text.

There are several ways to do this, so let's try a few of them out. We will program two methods from scratch to build our intuition, and then check how spaCy handles tokenization.

Intuitive – split by whitespace

The following lines of code simply segment or *split* the entire text body on space ' ':

```
words = text.split()
print(len(words))

    107431
```

Let's preview a rather large segment from our list of tokens:

```
print(words[90:200])   #start with the first chapter, ignoring the index for
now
    ['To', 'Sherlock', 'Holmes', 'she', 'is', 'always', 'THE', 'woman.',
'I', 'have', 'seldom', 'heard', 'him', 'mention', 'her', 'under', 'any',
'other', 'name.', 'In', 'his', 'eyes', 'she', 'eclipses', 'and',
'predominates', 'the', 'whole', 'of', 'her', 'sex.', 'It', 'was', 'not',
'that', 'he', 'felt', 'any', 'emotion', 'akin', 'to', 'love', 'for',
'Irene', 'Adler.', 'All', 'emotions,', 'and', 'that', 'one',
'particularly,', 'were', 'abhorrent', 'to', 'his', 'cold,', 'precise',
'but', 'admirably', 'balanced', 'mind.', 'He', 'was,', 'I', 'take', 'it,',
'the', 'most', 'perfect', 'reasoning', 'and', 'observing', 'machine',
'that', 'the', 'world', 'has', 'seen,', 'but', 'as', 'a', 'lover', 'he',
'would', 'have', 'placed', 'himself', 'in', 'a', 'false', 'position.',
```

```
'He', 'never', 'spoke', 'of', 'the', 'softer', 'passions,', 'save', 'with',
'a', 'gibe', 'and', 'a', 'sneer.', 'They', 'were', 'admirable', 'things',
'for']
```

The way punctuation is split here is not desirable. It often appears with the word itself, such as the full stop at end of `Adler.` and a comma being part of `emotions,`. Quite often we want words to be separated from punctuation, because words convey a lot more meaning than punctuation in most datasets.

Let's look at a shorter example:

```
'red-headed woman on the street'.split()
```

The following is the output from the preceding code:

```
['red-headed', 'woman', 'on', 'the', 'street']
```

Note how the words *red-headed* were not split. This is something we may or may not want to keep. We will come back to this, so keep this in mind.

One way to tackle this punctuation challenge is to simply extract words and discard everything else. This means that we will discard all non-ASCII characters and punctuation.

The hack – splitting by word extraction

Word extraction can be done in several ways. In turn, we can use word extraction for splitting the words into tokens. We will look at Regex, or Regular Expressions for doing word extractions. It is a pattern driven string search mechanism where the pattern grammar is defined by the user.

Introducing Regexes

Regular expressions can be a little challenging at first, but they are very powerful. They are generic abstractions, and work across multiple languages beyond Python:

```
import re
re.split('\W+', 'Words, words, words.')
> ['Words', 'words', 'words', '']
```

Tidying your Text

The regular expression \W+ means *a word character (A-Z etc.) repeated one or more times:*

```
words_alphanumeric = re.split('\W+', text)
print(len(words_alphanumeric), len(words))
```

The output of the preceding code is (109111, 107431).

Let's preview the words we extracted:

```
print(words_alphanumeric[90:200])
```

The following is the output we got from the preceding code:

```
['BOHEMIA', 'I', 'To', 'Sherlock', 'Holmes', 'she', 'is', 'always',
'THE', 'woman', 'I', 'have', 'seldom', 'heard', 'him', 'mention', 'her',
'under', 'any', 'other', 'name', 'In', 'his', 'eyes', 'she', 'eclipses',
'and', 'predominates', 'the', 'whole', 'of', 'her', 'sex', 'It', 'was',
'not', 'that', 'he', 'felt', 'any', 'emotion', 'akin', 'to', 'love', 'for',
'Irene', 'Adler', 'All', 'emotions', 'and', 'that', 'one', 'particularly',
'were', 'abhorrent', 'to', 'his', 'cold', 'precise', 'but', 'admirably',
'balanced', 'mind', 'He', 'was', 'I', 'take', 'it', 'the', 'most',
'perfect', 'reasoning', 'and', 'observing', 'machine', 'that', 'the',
'world', 'has', 'seen', 'but', 'as', 'a', 'lover', 'he', 'would', 'have',
'placed', 'himself', 'in', 'a', 'false', 'position', 'He', 'never',
'spoke', 'of', 'the', 'softer', 'passions', 'save', 'with', 'a', 'gibe',
'and', 'a', 'sneer', 'They', 'were', 'admirable']
```

We notice how Adler no longer has the punctuation mark alongside it. This is what we wanted. Mission accomplished?

What was the trade-off we made here? To understand that, let's look at another example:

```
words_break = re.split('\W+', "Isn't he coming home for dinner with the red-headed girl?")
print(words_break)
```

The following is the output we got from the preceding code:

```
['Isn', 't', 'he', 'coming', 'home', 'for', 'dinner', 'with', 'the',
'red', 'headed', 'girl', '']
```

[28]

We have split `Isn't` to `Isn` and `t`. This isn't good if you're working with, say, email or Twitter data, because you would have a lot more of these contractions and abbreviations. As a minor annoyance, we have an extra empty token, `' '`, at the end. Similarly, because we neglected punctuation, `red-headed` is broken into two words: `red` and `headed`. We have no straightforward way to restore this connection if we are only given the tokenized version.

We can write custom rules in our tokenization strategy to cover most of these edge cases. Or, we can use something that has already been written for us.

spaCy for tokenization

spaCy loads the English *model* using the preceding `.load` syntax. This tells spaCy what rules, logic, weights, and other information to use:

```
%%time
import spacy
# python -m spacy download en
# uncomment above line to download the model
nlp = spacy.load('en')
```

While we use only `'en'` or English examples in this book, spaCy supports these features for more languages. I have used their multi-language tokenizer for Hindi as well, and have been satisfied with the same:

> The `%%time` syntax measures the CPU and Wall time at your runtime execution for the cell in a Jupyter not ebook.

```
doc = nlp(text)
```

This creates a spaCy object, `doc`. The object stores pre-computed linguistic features, including tokens. Some NLP libraries, especially in the Java and C ecosystem, compute linguistic features such as tokens, lemmas, and parts of speech when that specific function is called. Instead, spaCy computes them all at initialization when the `text` is passed to it.

> spaCy pre-computes most linguistic features – all you have to do is retrieve them from the object.

Tidying your Text

We can retrieve them by calling the object iterator. In the following code, we call the iterator and *list* it:

```
print(list(doc)[150:200])
```

The following is the output from the preceding code:

```
[whole, of, her, sex, ., It, was, not, that, he, felt,
   , any, emotion, akin, to, love, for, Irene, Adler, ., All, emotions, ,,
and, that,
   , one, particularly, ,, were, abhorrent, to, his, cold, ,, precise, but,
   , admirably, balanced, mind, ., He, was, ,, I, take, it, ,]
```

Conveniently, spaCy tokenizes all punctuation and words. They are returned as individual tokens. Let's try the example that we didn't like earlier:

```
words = nlp("Isn't he coming home for dinner with the red-headed girl?")
print([token for token in words])
> [Is, n't, he, coming, home, for, dinner, with, the, red, -, headed, girl, ?]
```

Here are the observations:

- spaCy got the `Isn't` split correct: `Is` and `n't`.
- `red-headed` was broken into three tokens: `red`, `-`, and `headed`. Since the punctuation information isn't lost, we can restore the original `red-headed` token if we want to.

How does the spaCy tokenizer work?

The simplest explanation is from the spaCy docs (`spacy-101`) itself.

First, the raw text is split on whitespace characters, similar to text.split (' '). Then, the tokenizer processes the text from left to right. On each substring, it performs two checks:

- *Does the substring match a tokenizer exception rule?* For example, *don't* does not contain whitespace, but should be split into two tokens, *do* and *n't*, while *U.K.* should always remain one token.
- *Can a prefix, suffix, or infix be split off?* For example, punctuation such as commas, periods, hyphens, or quotes:

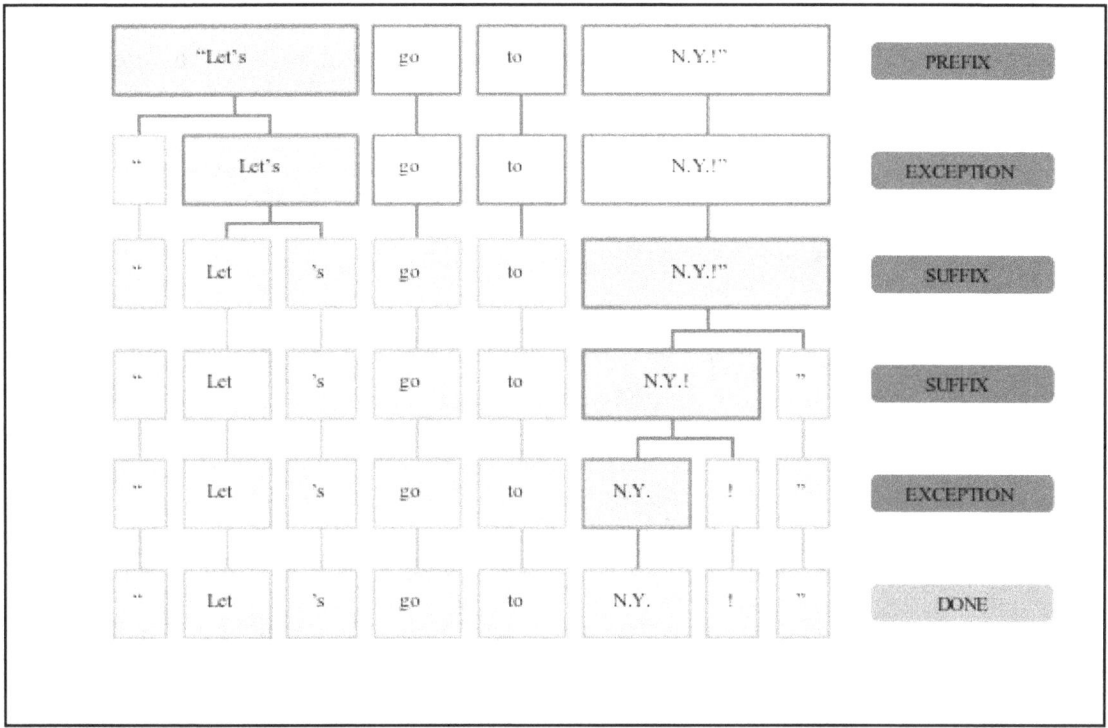

Sentence tokenization

We can also use spaCy to extract one sentence at a time, instead of one word at a time:

```
sentences = list(doc.sents)
print(sentences[14:18])
```

The following is the output from the preceding code:

```
[she is always THE woman., I have seldom heard
  him mention her under any other name., In his eyes she eclipse
  and predominates the whole of her sex., It was not that he felt
  any emotion akin to love for Irene Adler.]
```

Stop words removal and case change

These simple ideas are widespread and fairly effective for a lot of tasks. They are particularly useful in reducing the number of unique tokens in a document for your processing.

Tidying your Text

spaCy has already marked each token as a stop word or not and stored it in the `is_stop` attribute of each token. This makes it very handy for text cleaning. Let's take a quick look:

```
sentence_example = "the AI/AGI uprising cannot happen without the progress of NLP"
[(token, token.is_stop, token.is_punct) for token in nlp(sentence_example)]

   [(the, True, False),
    (AI, False, False),
    (/, False, True),
    (AGI, True, False),
    (uprising, False, False),
    (can, True, False),
    (not, True, False),
    (happen, False, False),
    (without, True, False),
    (the, True, False),
    (progress, False, False),
    (of, True, False),
    (NLP, True, False)]
```

Getting back to our Sherlock example, let's take a look at the first few lines and whether they count as stop words or not:

```
for token in doc[:5]:
    print(token, token.is_stop, token.is_punct)

Output:
    THE False False
    ADVENTURES False False
    OF False False
    SHERLOCK False False
    HOLMES False False
```

Interesting – while *the* and *of* were marked as stop words, `THE` and `OF` were not. This is not a bug, but by design. spaCy doesn't remove words that are different because of their capitals or title case automatically.

Instead, we can force this behavior by converting our original text to lowercase before we pass it to spaCy:

```
text_lower = text.lower()   # native python function
doc_lower = nlp(text_lower)
for token in doc_lower[:5]:
    print(token, token.is_stop)

Output:
```

```
the True
adventures False
of True
sherlock False
holmes False
```

Let's look at what stop words exist in the spaCy dictionary, and then how to extend the same programmatically:

```
from spacy.lang.en.stop_words import STOP_WORDS
f'spaCy has a dictionary of {len(list(STOP_WORDS))} stop words'

    'spaCy has a dictionary of 305 stop words'
```

We want to expand the stop words dictionary according to our domain and problem. For instance, if you were using this code to process the text of an NLP book, we might want to add words such as NLP, *Processing*, AGI, *Data*, and so on to the stop words list.

spaCy has an intuitive .add() API to do this:

```
domain_stop_words = ["NLP", "Processing", "AGI"]
for word in domain_stop_words:
    STOP_WORDS.add(word)
```

Let's try running the same example as earlier with these added stop words:

```
[(token, token.is_stop, token.is_punct) for token in nlp(sentence_example)]
```

The following is the output from running the preceding code:

```
        [(the, True, False),
        (AI, False, False),
        (/, False, True),
        (AGI, True, False),
        (uprising, False, False),
        (can, True, False),
        (not, True, False),
        (happen, False, False),
        (without, True, False),
        (the, True, False),
        (progress, False, False),
        (of, True, False),
        (NLP, True, False)]
```

Exactly as expected, NLP and AGI are now marked as stop words too.

Let's pull out string tokens which are not stop words into a Python list or similar data structure.

Tidying your Text

Some NLP tasks that come after text pre-processing expect string tokens and not spaCy token objects as a datatype. Removing both stop words and punctuation here for demonstration:

```
[str(token) for token in nlp(sentence_example) if not token.is_stop and not token.is_punct]
  ['AI', 'uprising', 'happen', 'progress']
```

Or just removing stop words, while retaining punctuation:

```
[str(token) for token in nlp(sentence_example) if not token.is_stop]
  ['AI'], '/', 'uprising', 'happen', 'progress']
```

Stemming and lemmatization

Stemming and lemmatization are very two very popular ideas that are used to reduce the vocabulary size of your corpus.

> **Stemming** *usually refers to a crude heuristic process that chops off the ends of words in the hope of achieving this goal correctly most of the time, and often includes the removal of derivational affixes.*
>
> **Lemmatization** *usually refers to doing things properly with the use of a vocabulary and morphological analysis of words, normally aiming to remove inflectional endings only and to return the base or dictionary form of a word, which is known as the lemma.*
>
> *If confronted with the token saw, stemming might return just s, whereas lemmatization would attempt to return either see or saw, depending on whether the use of the token was as a verb or a noun.*
>
> *- Dr. Christopher Manning et al, 2008,* [IR-Book]
> *(Chris Manning is a Professor in machine learning at the Departments of Computer Science and Linguistics at Stanford University)*

spaCy for lemmatization

spaCy only supports lemmatization. As discussed by spaCy creator Matt Honnibal in `issue #327` on GitHub, stemmers are rarely a good idea.

We want to treat meet/NOUN differently from meeting/VERB. Unlike Stanford NLTK, which was created to *teach and introduce* as many NLP ideas as possible, spaCy takes an opinionated stand against stemming.

spaCy does lemmatization for you by default when you process the text with the nlp object. This information is stored in the lemma attribute for each token. spaCy stores the internal hash or identifier, which spaCy stores in token.lemma. This numerical hash has no meaning for us. This numerical representation helps spaCy access and manipulate information much faster than its other Pythonic components.

An underscore at the attribute end, such as lemma_, tells spaCy that we are looking for something that is human-readable:

```
lemma_sentence_example = "Their Apples & Banana fruit salads are amazing.
Would you like meeting me at the cafe?"
[(token, token.lemma_, token.lemma, token.pos_ ) for token in
nlp(lemma_sentence_example)]

Printing this gives the following output:

  [(Their, '-PRON-', 561228191312463089, 'ADJ'),
   (Apples, 'apples', 14374618037326464786, 'PROPN'),
   (&, '&', 15473034735919704609, 'CCONJ'),
   (Banana, 'banana', 2525716904149915114, 'PROPN'),
   (fruit, 'fruit', 17674554054627885835, 'NOUN'),
   (salads, 'salad', 16382906660984395826, 'NOUN'),
   (are, 'be', 10382539506755952630, 'VERB'),
   (amazing, 'amazing', 12968186374132960503, 'ADJ'),
   (., '.', 12646065887601541794, 'PUNCT'),
   (Would, 'would', 6992604926141104606, 'VERB'),
   (you, '-PRON-', 561228191312463089, 'PRON'),
   (like, 'like', 18194338103975822726, 'VERB'),
   (meeting, 'meet', 6880656908171229526, 'VERB'),
   (me, '-PRON-', 561228191312463089, 'PRON'),
   (at, 'at', 11667289587015813222, 'ADP'),
   (the, 'the', 7425985699627899538, 'DET'),
   (cafe, 'cafe', 10569699879655997926, 'NOUN'),
   (?, '?', 8205403955989537350, 'PUNCT')]
```

There's quite a few things going on here. Let's discuss them.

-PRON-

spaCy has a slightly annoying lemma (recall that lemma is the output of lemmatization): -PRON-. This is used as the lemma for all pronouns such as `Their`, `you`, `me`, and `I`. Other NLP tools lemmatize these to `I` instead of a placeholder, such as `-PRON-`.

Case-insensitive

While checking for stop words, spaCy did not automatically lowercase our input. On the other hand, lemmatization does this for us. It converted "Apple" to "apple" and "Banana" to "banana".

This is one of the ways spaCy makes our lives easier, though slightly inconsistent. While removing stop words, we want to preserve THE in "THE ADVENTURES OF SHERLOCK HOLMES" while removing *the* in "the street was black". The opposite is usually true in lemmatization; we care more about how the word was used in context and use a proper lemma accordingly.

Conversion – meeting to meet

Lemmatization is aware of the linguistic role that words play in context. "Meeting" is converted to "meet" because it's a verb. spaCy does expose part of speech tagging and other linguistic features for us to use. We will learn how to query those soon.

spaCy compared with NLTK and CoreNLP

The following is a comparison of the NLTK and CoreNLP:

Feature	Spacy	NLTK	CoreNLP
Native Python support/API	Y	Y	Y
Multi-language support	Y	Y	Y
Tokenization	Y	Y	Y
Part-of-speech tagging	Y	Y	Y
Sentence segmentation	Y	Y	Y
Dependency parsing	Y	N	Y
Entity recognition	Y	Y	Y
Integrated word vectors	Y	N	N
Sentiment analysis	Y	Y	Y
Coreference resolution	N	N	Y

Correcting spelling

One of the most frequently seen text challenges is correcting spelling errors. This is all the more true when data is entered by casual human users, for instance, shipping addresses or similar.

Let's look at an example. We want to correct Gujrat, Gujart, and other minor misspellings to Gujarat. There are several good ways to do this, depending on your dataset and level of expertise. We will discuss two or three popular ways, and discuss their pros and cons.

Before I begin, we need to pay homage to the legendary `Peter Norvig's Spell Correct`. It's still worth a read on how to *think* about solving a problem and *exploring* implementations. Even the way he refactors his code and writes functions is educational.

His spell-correction module is not the simplest or best way of doing this. I recommend two packages: one with a bias toward simplicity, one with a bias toward giving you all the knives, bells, and whistles to try:

- `FuzzyWuzzy` is easy to use. It gives a simple similarity score between two strings, capped to 100. Higher numbers mean that the words are more similar.
- `Jellyfish` supports six edit distance functions and four phonetic encoding options that you can use as per your use case.

FuzzyWuzzy

Let's see how we can use FuzzyWuzzy to correct our misspellings.

Use the following code to install FuzzyWuzzy on your machine:

```
import sys

!{sys.executable} -m pip install fuzzywuzzy
# alternative for 4-10x faster computation:

# !{sys.executable} -m pip install fuzzywuzzy[speedup]
```

Tidying your Text

FuzzyWuzzy has two main modules that will come in useful: fuzz and process. Let's import fuzz first:

```
from fuzzywuzzy import fuzz
# Trying the ratio and partial_ratio
fuzz.ratio("Electronic City Phase One", "Electronic City Phase One, Bangalore")
# 82
fuzz.partial_ratio("Electronic City Phase One", "Electronic City Phase One, Bangalore")
# 100
```

We can see how the ratio function is confused by the trailing `Bangalore` used in the preceding address, but really the two strings refer to the same address/entity. This is captured by `partial_ratio`.

Do you see how both `ratio` and `partial_ratio` are sensitive to the ordering of the words? This is useful for comparing addresses that follow some order. On the other hand, if we want to compare something else, for example, person names, it might give counter-intuitive results:

```
fuzz.ratio('Narendra Modi', 'Narendra D. Modi')
# 90
fuzz.partial_ratio('Narendra Modi', 'Narendra D. Modi')
# 77
```

As you can see, just because we had an extra `D.` token, our logic is not applicable anymore. We want something that is less order-sensitive. The authors of FuzzyWuzzy have us covered.

FuzzyWuzzy supports functions that tokenize our input on space and remove punctuation, numbers, and non-ASCII characters. This is then used to calculate similarity. Let's try this out:

```
fuzz.token_sort_ratio('Narendra Modi', 'Narendra D. Modi')
# 93
fuzz.token_set_ratio('Narendra Modi', 'Narendra D. Modi')
# 100
```

This will work perfectly for us. In case we have a list of options and we want to find the closest match(es), we can use the process module:

```
from fuzzywuzzy import process
query = 'Gujrat'

choices = ['Gujarat', 'Gujjar', 'Gujarat Govt.']
```

```
# Get a list of matches ordered by score, default limit to 5
print(process.extract(query, choices))
# [('Gujarat', 92), ('Gujarat Govt.', 75), ('Gujjar', 67)]

# If we want only the top one result to be # returned:
process.extractOne(query, choices)
# ('Gujarat', 92)
```

Let's look at another example. Here, we have `Bangalore` misspelled as `Banglore` – we are missing an `a`:

```
query = 'Banglore'
choices = ['Bangalore', 'Bengaluru']
print(process.extract(query, choices))
# [('Bangalore', 94), ('Bengaluru', 59)]
process.extractOne(query, choices)
# ('Bangalore', 94)
```

Let's take an example of a common search typo in online shopping. Users have misspelled `chilli` as `chili`; note the missing `l`:

```
query = 'chili'
choices = ['chilli', 'chilled', 'chilling']
print(process.extract(query, choices))
# [('chilli', 91), ('chilling', 77), ('chilled', 67)]
process.extractOne(query, choices)
# ('chilli', 91)
```

Jellyfish

Jellyfish supports reasonably fast implementations of almost all popular edit distance functions (Recall how the edit distance functions tell you how similar two sequences/strings are). While FuzzyWuzzy supported mainly Levenshtein distance, this package supports some more string comparison utilities:

- Levenshtein distance
- Damerau-Levenshtein distance
- Jaro distance
- Jaro-Winkler distance
- Match rating approach comparison
- Hamming distance

Additionally, it supports **phonetic encodings** for English.

Use the following code to install Jellyfish on your machine:

```
import sys
# !{sys.executable} -m pip install jellyfish
```

Let's try importing the package and setting up some examples to try out:

```
import jellyfish

correct_example = ('Narendra Modi', 'Narendra Modi')
damodardas_example = ('Narendra Modi', 'Narendra D. Modi')
modi_typo_example = ('Narendra Modi', 'Narendar Modi')
gujarat_typo_example = ('Gujarat', 'Gujrat')

examples = [correct_example, damodardas_example, modi_typo_example,
gujarat_typo_example]
```

We want to try multiple distance functions with all of our examples. The smarter thing to do is build a utility function for this. Let's do that now:

```
def calculate_distance(function, examples=examples):
    for ele in examples:
        print(f'{ele}: {function(*ele)}')
```

Note that `calculate_distance` takes the distance function as input. We can leave `examples` as implicitly picked from what we had declared previously in the global namespace.

Levenshtein distance, which is probably the most famous string similarity function, is sometimes synonymous with edit distance function, but we consider this to be a particular implementation of the edit distance family of functions:

```
calculate_distance(jellyfish.levenshtein_distance)
# ('Narendra Modi', 'Narendra Modi'): 0
# ('Narendra Modi', 'Narendra D. Modi'): 3
# ('Narendra Modi', 'Narendar Modi'): 2
# ('Gujarat', 'Gujrat'): 1
```

The Damerau–Levenshtein distance adds transpositions to the Levenshtein edit operations of insertion, deletion, and substitution. Let's try this out and see if it changes anything for us:

```
calculate_distance(jellyfish.damerau_levenshtein_distance)
# ('Narendra Modi', 'Narendra Modi'): 0
# ('Narendra Modi', 'Narendra D. Modi'): 3
# ('Narendra Modi', 'Narendar Modi'): 1
# ('Gujarat', 'Gujrat'): 1
```

We note that the `Narendra` and `Narendar` distance value changed from 3 to 2. This is because we now count at least `a` to be transposed with `r` or vice versa. The other character is a substitution, so 1+1 = 2.

The next distance function that we will try is hamming distance. This counts the minimum number of substitutions required to change one string into the other:

```
calculate_distance(jellyfish.hamming_distance)
# ('Narendra Modi', 'Narendra Modi'): 0
# ('Narendra Modi', 'Narendra D. Modi'): 7
# ('Narendra Modi', 'Narendar Modi'): 2
# ('Gujarat', 'Gujrat'): 4
```

Jaro and Jaro-Winkler return a value of similarity – and not dissimilarity. This means that the perfect match returns 1.0 and a totally unrelated match would tend to be 0:

```
calculate_distance(jellyfish.jaro_distance)
# ('Narendra Modi', 'Narendra Modi'): 1.0
# ('Narendra Modi', 'Narendra D. Modi'): 0.9375
# ('Narendra Modi', 'Narendar Modi'): 0.9743589743589745
# ('Gujarat', 'Gujrat'): 0.8968253968253969
```

Trying the other variation of Jaro similarity, that is, Jaro-Winkler, we get the following:

```
calculate_distance(jellyfish.jaro_winkler)
# ('Narendra Modi', 'Narendra Modi'): 1.0
# ('Narendra Modi', 'Narendra D. Modi'): 0.9625
# ('Narendra Modi', 'Narendar Modi'): 0.9846153846153847
# ('Gujarat', 'Gujrat'): 0.9277777777777778
```

These are extremely useful and diverse techniques. Yet, their overemphasis on written text creates one problem that is unique to English. We don't write English in the same way we speak. This means that we do not capture the range of all similarities. To solve this challenge, which is typically encountered in chatbots used by non-native English speakers, we can look at the phonetic similarity of words, which is what we will do next.

Phonetic word similarity

The way we say a word makes up its phonetics. Phonetics is the information of speech sounds. For instance, soul and sole sound identical in a lot of British-derived accents, such as Indian accents.

Quite often, words might be misspelled a little bit because the typist was trying to make it *sound right*. In this case, we leverage this phonetic information to map this typo back to the correct spelling.

What is a phonetic encoding?

We can convert a word into a representation of its pronunciation. Of course, this might vary by accents, and by the conversion technique as well.

Yet, over time, two or three popular ways have emerged so that we can do this. Each of these methods takes a single string and returns a coded representation. I encourage you to Google each of these terms:

- **American Soundex (the 1930s)**: Implemented in popular database software such as PostgreSQL, MySQL, and SQLite
- **NYSIIS (New York State Identification and Intelligence System) (the 1970s)**
- Metaphone (the 1990s)
- **Match rating codex (the early 2000s)**

Let's take a quick preview of the same:

```
jellyfish.soundex('Jellyfish')
# 'J412'
```

For NYSIIS, we will use the following:

```
jellyfish.nysiis('Jellyfish')
# 'JALYF'
```

Using the slightly more updated metaphone, we get the following output:

```
jellyfish.metaphone('Jellyfish')
# 'JLFX'
```

The matching rate codex gives us the following output:

```
jellyfish.match_rating_codex('Jellyfish')
# 'JLYFSH'
```

We can now use the string comparison utility that we saw earlier to compare two strings phonetically.

Metaphone + Levenshtein

For instance, `write` and `right` should have zero phonetic Levenshtein distance because they are pronounced in the same way. Let's try this out:

```
jellyfish.levenshtein_distance(jellyfish.metaphone('write'),
jellyfish.metaphone('right'))#
# 0
```

This worked as expected. Let's add some examples to our old examples list:

```
examples+= [('write', 'right'), ('Mangalore', 'Bangalore'), ('Delhi',
'Dilli')] # adding a few examples to show how cool this is
```

Let's encapsulate this into a utility function, like we did earlier. We will use two function parameters now: `phonetic_func` and `distance_func`:

```
def calculate_phonetic_distance(phonetic_func, distance_func,
examples=examples):
    print("Word\t\tSound\t\tWord\t\t\tSound\t\tPhonetic Distance")
    for ele in examples:
        correct, typo = ele[0], ele[1]
        phonetic_correct, phonetic_typo = phonetic_func(correct),
phonetic_func(typo)
        phonetic_distance = distance_func(phonetic_correct, phonetic_typo)
        print(f'{correct:<10}\t{phonetic_correct:<10}\t{typo:<20}\t{phonetic_typo:<
10}\t{phonetic_distance:<10}')
calculate_phonetic_distance(phonetic_func=jellyfish.metaphone,
distance_func=jellyfish.levenshtein_distance)
```

This returns the following table:

Word	Sound	Word	Sound	Phonetic Distance
Narendra Modi	NRNTR MT	Narendra Modi	NRNTR MT	0
Narendra Modi	NRNTR MT	Narendra D. Modi	NRNTR T MT	2
Narendra Modi	NRNTR MT	Narendar Modi	NRNTR MT	0
Gujarat	KJRT	Gujrat	KJRT	0
write	RT	right	RT	0
Mangalore	MNKLR	Bangalore	BNKLR	1
Delhi	TLH	Dilli	TL	1

Note that Delhi and Dilli are separated, which is not nice. On the other hand, Narendra and Narendar are marked as similar to zero edit distance, which is quite cool. Let's try a different technique and see how it goes.

Tidying your Text

American soundex

We note that the Soundex is aware of common similar-sounding words and gives them separate phonetic encoding. This allows us to separate `right` from `write`.

This will only work on American/English words though. Indian sounds such as `Narendra Modi` and `Narendra D. Modi` are now considered similar:

```
calculate_phonetic_distance(phonetic_func=jellyfish.soundex,
distance_func=jellyfish.levenshtein_distance)
```

Note the changes from the previous code in the following table:

```
Word              Sound        Word              Sound
Phonetic Distance
Narendra Modi     N653         Narendra Modi     N653          0
Narendra Modi     N653         Narendra D. Modi  N653          0
Narendra Modi     N653         Narendar Modi     N653          0
Gujarat           G263         Gujrat            G263          0
write             W630         right             R230          2
Mangalore         M524         Bangalore         B524          1
Delhi             D400         Dilli             D400          0
```

Runtime complexity

We now have the ability to find the correct spellings of words or mark them as similar. While processing a large corpus, we can extract all unique words and compare each token against every other token.

It would take $O(n^2)$, where n is the number of unique tokens in a corpus. This might make the process too slow for a large corpus.

The alternative is to use a standard dictionary and expand the same for your corpus. If the dictionary has m unique words, this process now will be $O(m*n)$.
Assuming that $m \ll n * m \ll n^2$, this will be much faster than the previous approach.

Cleaning a corpus with FlashText

But what about a web-scale corpus with millions of documents and a few thousand keywords? Regex can take several days to run over such exact searches because of its linear time complexity. How can we improve this?

We can use FlashText for this very specific use case:

- A few million documents with a few thousand keywords
- Exact keyword matches – either by replacing or searching for the presence of those keywords

Of course, there are several different possible solutions to this problem. I recommend this for its simplicity and focus on solving one problem. It does not require us to learn new syntax or set up specific tools such as ElasticSearch.

The following table gives you a comparison of using Flashtext versus compiled regex for searching:

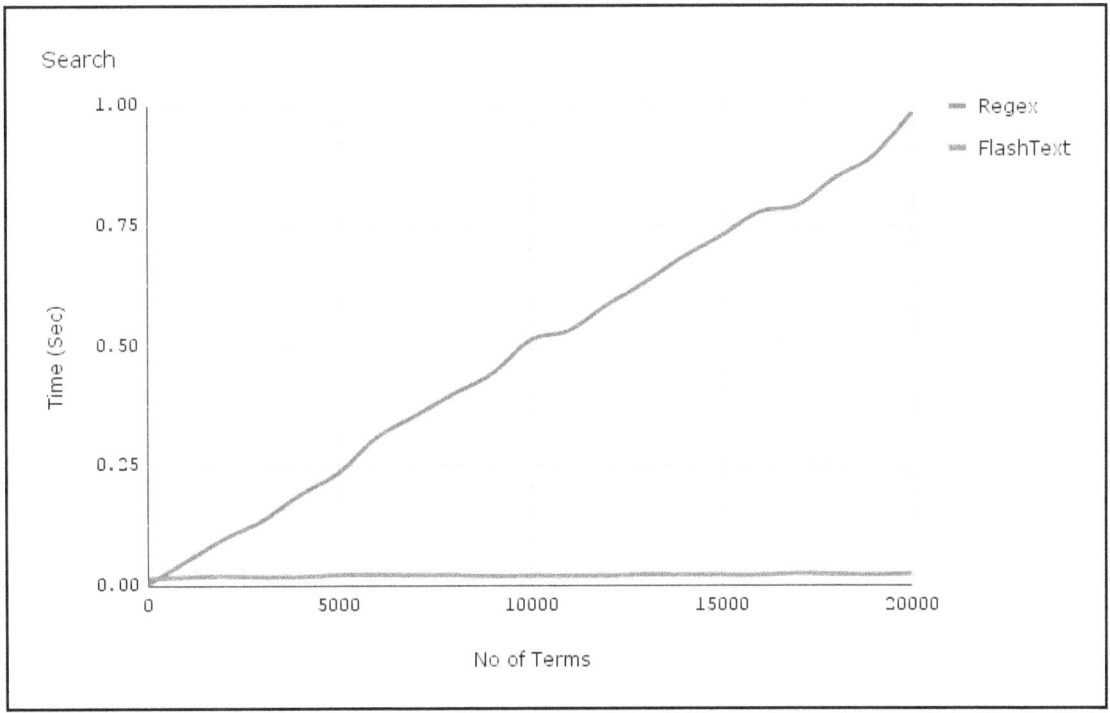

Tidying your Text

The following tables gives you a comparison of using FlashText versus compiled regex for substitutions:

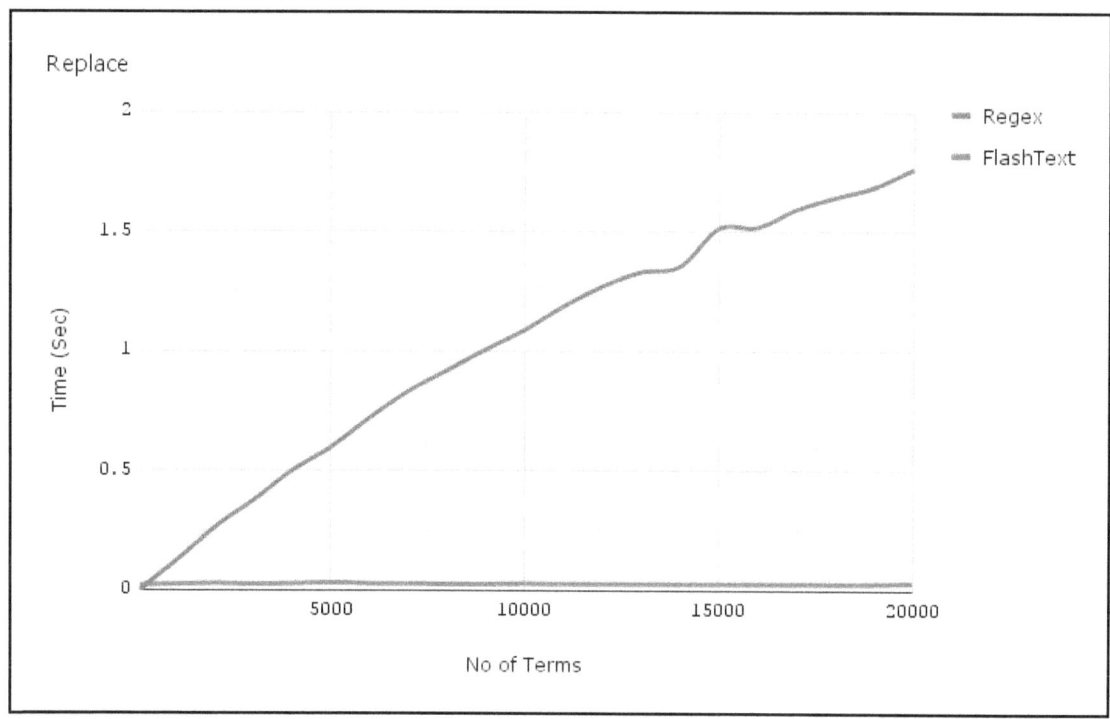

We note that while the time taken by Regex scales almost linearly, Flashtext is relatively flat. Now, we know that we need Flashtext for speed and scale. FlashText has seen a lot of love from the community. Adopters include `NLProc` – the NLP Preprocessing Toolkit from the National Institute of Health.

Follow these instructions to install FlashText onto your machine.

First, we will install pip on our conda environment. We will do this from our notebook:

```
# import sys
# !{sys.executable} -m pip install flashtext
```

The FlashText source code is available on GitHub (`https://github.com/PacktPublishing/Natural-Language-Processing-with-Python-Quick-Start/tree/master/Chapter02`), and the documents are pretty easy to navigate and use. We will only consider two basic examples here. Let's figure out the syntax for finding keywords that exist in a corpus:

```
from flashtext.keyword import KeywordProcessor
keyword_processor = KeywordProcessor()
keyword_processor.add_keyword('Delhi', 'NCR') # notice we are adding tuples here
keyword_processor.add_keyword('Bombay', 'Mumbai')
keywords_found = keyword_processor.extract_keywords('I love the food in Delhi and the people in Bombay')
keywords_found
# ['NCR', 'Mumbai']
```

How about we replace them now?

```
from flashtext.keyword import KeywordProcessor
keyword_processor = KeywordProcessor()
keyword_processor.add_keyword('Delhi', 'NCR')
keyword_processor.add_keyword('Bombay', 'Mumbai')
replaced_sentence = keyword_processor.replace_keywords('I love the food in Delhi and the people in Bombay')
replaced_sentence
# 'I love the food in NCR and the people in Mumbai'
```

Unfortunately, FlashText only supports English for the time being. Regex can search for keywords based on special characters such as ^, $, *, \d, which are not supported in FlashText. So, to match partial words such as `word\dvec`, we would still have to use regex. However, FlashText is still excellent for extracting complete words like `word2vec`.

Summary

This chapter covered a lot of new ground. We started by performing linguistic processing on our text. We met **spaCy**, which we will continue to dive deeper into as we move on in this book. We covered the following foundational ideas from linguistics, tokenization doing this with and without spaCy, stop word removal, case standardization, lemmatization (we skipped stemming) – using spaCy and its peculiarities such as -*PRON-*

But what do we do with spaCy, other than text cleaning? Can we build something? Yes!

Not only can we extend our simple linguistics based text cleaning using spaCy pipelines but also do parts of speech tagging, named entity recognition, and other common tasks. We will look at this in the next chapter.

We looked at spelling correction or the closest word match problem. We discussed **FuzzyWuzzy** and **Jellyfish** in this context. To ensure that we can scale beyond more than a few hundred keywords, we also looked at **FlashText**. I encourage you to dive deeper into any of these excellent libraries to learn about the best software engineering practices.

In the next chapter, we will tie all these together with other linguistic tools to build an end-to-end toy program.

3
Leveraging Linguistics

In this chapter, we are going to pick up a simple use case and see how we can solve it. Then, we repeat this task again, but on a slightly different text corpus.

This helps us learn about build intuition when using linguistics in NLP. I will be using spaCy here, but you are free to use NLTK or an equivalent. There are programmatic differences in their APIs and styles, but the underlying theme remains the same.

In the previous chapter, we had our first taste of handling free text. Specifically, we learned how to tokenize text into words and sentences, pattern match with regex, and make fast substitutions.

By doing all of this, we operated with text on a *string* as the main representation. In this chapter, we will use *language* and *grammar* as the main representations.

In this chapter, we will learn about the following topics:

- spaCy, the natural language library for industrial use
- The NLP pipeline, and a bit of English grammar
- Real-life examples regarding what we can do with linguistics

Linguistics and NLP

This section is dedicated to introducing you to the ideas and tools that have been around during several decades of linguistics. The most traditional way to introduce this is to take an idea, talk about it at length, and then put all of this together.

Here, I am going to do this the other way around. We will solve two problems and, in the process, look at the tools we will be using. Instead of talking to you about a number 8 spanner, I am giving you a car engine and the tools, and I will introduce the tools as I use them.

Leveraging Linguistics

Most NLP tasks are solved in a sequential pipeline, with the results from one component feeding into the next.

There is a wide variety of data structures that are used to store pipeline results and intermediate steps. Here, for simplicity, I am going to use only the data structures that are already in spaCy and the native Python ones like lists and dictionaries.

Here, we will tackle the following real-life inspired challenges:

- Redacting names from any document, for example, for GDPR compliance
- Making quizzes from any text, for example, from a Wikipedia article

Getting started

You can install spaCy via `conda` or `pip`. Since I am in a `conda` environment, I will use the `conda` installation, as follows:

```
# !conda install -y spacy
# !pip install spacy
```

Let's download the English language model provided by spaCy. We are going to use `en_core_web_lg` (the `lg` at the end stands for *large*). This means that this is the most comprehensive and best performing model that spaCy has released for general-purpose use.

You only need to do this once:

```
!python -m spacy download en_core_web_lg
```

If you run into any errors when you download this, you can use the smaller model instead.

For Windows Shell, you can use `python -m spacy download en` as the administrator. From a Linux Terminal, you can use `sudo python -m spacy download en`.

Let's get the imports out of the way:

```
import spacy
from spacy import displacy # for visualization
nlp = spacy.load('en_core_web_lg')
spacy.__version__
```

The version I am using here is `version 2.0.11` from conda, but you can use any version above 2.0.x.

Introducing textacy

Textacy is a very underappreciated set of tools that revolves around spaCy. Its tagline tells you exactly what it does: *NLP, before and after spaCy*. It implements tools that use spaCy under the hood, ranging from data-streaming utilities for production use to higher level text-clustering functions.

You can install textacy via `pip` or `conda`. On `conda`, it's available on the `conda-forge` channel instead of the main `conda` channel. We've done this by adding a `-c` flag and the channel name after that:

```
# !conda install -c conda-forge textacy
# !pip install textacy
import textacy
```

Now that we have the set up and have installation out of our way, let's get ready to tackle our challenge in the following section.

Redacting names with named entity recognition

The challenge for this section is to replace all human names with [REDACTED] in free text.

Let's imagine that you are a new engineer at the European Bank Co. In preparation for the **General Data Processing Regulation** (**GDPR**), the bank is scrubbing off names of their customers from all of their old records and special internal communications like email and memos. They ask you to do this.

The first way you can do this is to look up the names of your customers and match each of them against all of your emails. This can be painfully slow and error-prone. For example, let's say the bank has a customer named John D'Souza – you might simply refer to him as DSouza in an email, so an exact match for D'Souza will never be scrubbed from the system.

Here, we will use an automatic NLP technique to assist us. We will parse all of our emails from spaCy and simply replace everyone's names with the token [REDACTED]. This will be at least 5-10 times faster than matching millions of substrings against millions of substrings.

Leveraging Linguistics

We will use a small excerpt from the *Harry Potter and Chamber of Secrets*, talking about flu as an example:

```
text = "Madam Pomfrey, the nurse, was kept busy by a sudden spate of colds
among the staff and students. Her Pepperup potion worked instantly, though
it left the drinker smoking at the ears for several hours afterward. Ginny
Weasley, who had been looking pale, was bullied into taking some by Percy."
```

Let's parse the text with spaCy. This runs the entire NLP pipeline:

```
doc = nlp(text)
```

`doc` now contains a parsed version of the text. We can use it to do anything we want! For example, the following command will print out all the named entities that were detected:

```
for entity in doc.ents:
    print(f"{entity.text} ({entity.label_})")

Pomfrey (PERSON)
Pepperup (ORG)
several hours (TIME)
Ginny Weasley (PERSON)
Percy (PERSON)
```

The spaCy object `doc` has an attribute called `ents` which stores all detected entities. To find this, spaCy has done a few things behind the scenes for us, for example:

- **Sentence segmentation**, to break the long text into smaller sentences
- **Tokenization**, to break each sentence into individual words or tokens
- **Removed stop words**, to remove words like *a, an, the,* and *of*
- **NER** for statistical techniques in order to find out which *entities* are there in the text and label them with the entity's type

Let's take a quick look at the `doc` object, too:

```
doc.ents
> (Pomfrey, Pepperup, several hours, Ginny Weasley, Percy)
```

The `doc` object has a specific object called `ents`, which is short for entities. We can use these to look up all of the entities in our text. Additionally, each entity has a label:

In spaCy, all information is stored by numeric hashing. Therefore, `entity.label` will be a numeric entry like 378, while `entity.label_` will be human-readable, for example, PERSON.

Chapter 3

```
entity.label, entity.label_
> (378, 'PERSON')
```

In spaCy, all human-readable labels can also be explained using the simple `spacy.explain(label)` syntax:

```
spacy.explain('GPE')
> 'Countries, cities, states'
```

Using spaCy's NER, let's write a simple function to replace each PERSON name with [REDACTED]:

```
def redact_names(text):
    doc = nlp(text)
    redacted_sentence = []
    for token in doc:
        if token.ent_type_ == "PERSON":
            redacted_sentence.append("[REDACTED]")
        else:
            redacted_sentence.append(token.string)
    return "".join(redacted_sentence)
```

The function takes in text as a string and parses it in the `doc` object using the `nlp` object, which we loaded earlier. Then, it traverses each token in the document (remember tokenization?). Each token is added to a list. If the token has the entity type of a person, it is replaced with [REDACTED] instead.

At the end, we reconstruct the original sentence by converting this list back into a string:

As an exercise, try completing this challenge in-place by editing the original string itself instead of creating a new string.

```
redact_names(text)

> 'Madam [REDACTED], the nurse, was kept busy by a sudden spate of colds
among the staff and students. Her Pepperup potion worked instantly, though
it left the drinker smoking at the ears for several hours afterward.
[REDACTED][REDACTED], who had been looking pale, was bullied into taking
some by [REDACTED]
```

The preceding output is still a leaky faucet if you are trying to make GDPR-compliant edits. By using two [REDACTED] blocks instead of one, we are disclosing the number of words in a name. This can be seriously harmful if we were to use this in some other context, for example, redacting locations or organization names.

[53]

Leveraging Linguistics

Let's fix this:

```
def redact_names(text):
    doc = nlp(text)
    redacted_sentence = []
    for ent in doc.ents:
        ent.merge()
    for token in doc:
        if token.ent_type_ == "PERSON":
            redacted_sentence.append("[REDACTED]")
        else:
            redacted_sentence.append(token.string)
    return "".join(redacted_sentence)
```

We do this by merging entities separately from the pipeline. Notice the two extra lines of code which call `ent.merge()` on all entities found. The `ent.merge()` function combines all of the tokens in each *entity* into one single token. This is why it needs to be called on each entity:

```
redact_names(text)
> 'Madam [REDACTED], the nurse, was kept busy by a sudden spate of colds
among the staff and students. Her Pepperup potion worked instantly, though
it left the drinker smoking at the ears for several hours afterward.
[REDACTED], who had been looking pale, was bullied into taking some by
[REDACTED].
```

This output, in practice, can still be incomplete. You might want to remove the gender here, for example, *Madam*. Since we are already disclosing the designation, which is *nurse*, giving away the gender makes it easier to infer for people (or even machines) who are reading this document.

Exercise: Remove any gender pronouns in reference to names.
Hint: Look up the co-reference resolution to help you with this.

Entity types

spaCy supports the following entity types in the large language model that we loaded in the `nlp` object:

Type	Description
PERSON	People, including fictional people
NORP	Nationalities or religious or political groups
FAC	Buildings, airports, highways, bridges, and so on
ORG	Companies, agencies, institutions, and so on
GPE	Countries, cities, states
LOC	Non-GPE locations, mountain ranges, bodies of water
PRODUCT	Objects, vehicles, foods, and so on (not services)
EVENT	Named hurricanes, battles, wars, sports events, and so on
WORK_OF_ART	Titles of books, songs, and so on
LAW	Named documents made into laws
LANGUAGE	Any named language
DATE	Absolute or relative dates or periods
TIME	Times smaller than a day
PERCENT	Percentage, including %
MONEY	Monetary values, including unit
QUANTITY	Measurements, such as weight or distance
ORDINAL	*First*, *second*, and so on
CARDINAL	Numerals that do not fall under another type

Let's look at some examples of the preceding entity types in real-world sentences. We will also use `spacy.explain()` on all of the entities to build a quick mental model of how these things work.

Given how lazy I am, I will write a function that I can reuse again and again so that I can simply focus on learning and not debugging code for different examples:

```
def explain_text_entities(text):
    doc = nlp(text)
    for ent in doc.ents:
        print(f'{ent}, Label: {ent.label_}, {spacy.explain(ent.label_)}')
```

Let's give it a spin with a few simple examples to begin with:

```
explain_text_entities('Tesla has gained 20% market share in the months
since')

Tesla, Label: ORG, Companies, agencies, institutions, etc.
20%, Label: PERCENT, Percentage, including "%"
the months, Label: DATE, Absolute or relative dates or periods
```

Let's look at a slightly longer sentence and Eastern example:

```
explain_text_entities('Taj Mahal built by Mughal Emperor Shah Jahan stands
tall on the banks of Yamuna in modern day Agra, India')

Taj Mahal, Label: PERSON, People, including fictional
Mughal, Label: NORP, Nationalities or religious or political groups
Shah Jahan, Label: PERSON, People, including fictional
Yamuna, Label: LOC, Non-GPE locations, mountain ranges, bodies of water
Agra, Label: GPE, Countries, cities, states
India, Label: GPE, Countries, cities, states
```

Interesting – the model got `Taj Mahal` wrong. Taj Mahal is obviously a world-famous monument. However, the model has made a believable mistake, because `Taj Mahal` was also the stage name of a blues musician.

In most production use cases, we *fine-tune* the built-in spaCy models for specific languages using our own annotations. This will teach the model that Taj Mahal, for us, is almost always a monument and not a blues musician.

Let's see if the model repeats these mistakes in other examples:

```
explain_text_entities('Ashoka was a great Indian king')
Ashoka, Label: PERSON, People, including fictional
Indian, Label: NORP, Nationalities or religious or political groups
```

Let's try a different sentence with a different meaning of Ashoka:

```
explain_text_entities('The Ashoka University sponsors the Young India
Fellowship')
Ashoka University, Label: ORG, Companies, agencies, institutions, etc.
the Young India Fellowship, Label: ORG, Companies, agencies, institutions,
etc.
```

Here, spaCy is able to leverage the word `University` to infer that Ashoka is a name of an organization and not King Ashoka from Indian history.

It has also figured out that `Young India Fellowship` is one logical entity and has not tagged `India` as a location.

It helps to see a few examples such as these ones to form a mental model regarding what the limits of what we can and cannot do are.

Automatic question generation

Can you automatically convert a sentence into a question?

For instance, *Martin Luther King Jr. was a civil rights activist and skilled orator.* to *Who was Martin Luther King Jr.?*

Notice that when we convert a sentence into a question, the answer might not be in the original sentence anymore. To me, the answer to that question might be something different, and that's fine. We are not aiming for answers here.

Part-of-speech tagging

Sometimes, we want to pull out keywords or keyphrases from a larger body of text quickly. This helps us mentally paint a picture of what this text is about. This is particularly helpful in the analysis of texts, like long emails or essays.

As a quick hack, we can pull out all relevant *nouns*. This is because most keywords are in fact nouns of some form:

```
example_text = 'Bansoori is an Indian classical instrument. Tom plays Bansoori and Guitar.'

doc = nlp(example_text)
```

We need noun chunks. Noun chunks are noun phrases – not single words, but a short phrase which describes the noun. For example, *the blue skies* or *the world's largest conglomerate*.

Leveraging Linguistics

To get the noun chunks from a document, simply iterate over `doc.noun_chunks`:

```
for idx, sentence in enumerate(doc.sents):
    for noun in sentence.noun_chunks:
        print(f'sentence{idx+1}', noun)

sentence1 Bansoori
sentence1 an Indian classical instrument
sentence2 Tom
sentence2 Bansoori
sentence2 Guitar
```

Our example text has two sentences, and we can pull out noun phrase chunks from each sentence. We will pull out noun phrases instead of single words. This means that we are able to pull out *an Indian classical instrument* as one noun. This is quite useful, and we will see why in a moment.

Next, let's take a quick look at all of the parts-of-speech tags in our example text. We will use verbs and adjectives to write some simple question-generating logic:

```
for token in doc:
    print(token, token.pos_, token.tag_)

Bansoori PROPN NNP
is VERB VBZ
an DET DT
Indian ADJ JJ
classical ADJ JJ
instrument NOUN NN
. PUNCT .
Tom PROPN NNP
plays VERB VBZ
Bansoori PROPN NNP
and CCONJ CC
Guitar PROPN NNP
. PUNCT .
```

Notice that here, *instrument* is tagged as a NOUN, while *Indian* and *classical* are tagged as adjectives. This makes sense. Additionally, *Bansoori* and *Guitar* are tagged as PROPN, or proper nouns.

Common nouns versus proper nouns: Nouns name people, places, and things. Common nouns name general items such as waiter, jeans, and country. Proper nouns name specific things such as Roger, Levi's, and India.

[58]

Creating a ruleset

Quite often when using linguistics, you will be writing custom rules. Here is one data structure suggestion to help you store these rules: a list of dictionaries. Each dictionary in turn can have elements ranging from simple string lists to lists of strings. Avoid nesting a list of dictionaries inside a dictionary:

```
ruleset = [
    {
        'id': 1,
        'req_tags': ['NNP', 'VBZ', 'NN'],
    },
    {
        'id': 2,
        'req_tags': ['NNP', 'VBZ'],
    }
]
```

Here, I have written two rules. Each rule is simply a collection of part-of-speech tags that has been stored under the `req_tags` key. Each rule is comprised of all of the tags that I will look for in a particular sentence.

Depending on `id`, I will use a hardcoded question template to generate my questions. In practice, you can and should move the question template to your ruleset.

Next, I need a function to pull out all of the tokens that match a particular tag. We do this by simply iterating over the entire list of and matching each token against the target tag:

```
def get_pos_tag(doc, tag):
    return [tok for tok in doc if tok.tag_ == tag]
```

On runtime complexity:

This is slow O(n). As an exercise, can you think of a way to reduce this to O(1)?
Hint: You can precompute some results and store them, but at the cost of more memory consumption.

Next, I am going to write a function to use the preceding ruleset, and also use a question template.

Here is the broad outline that I will follow for each sentence:

- For each rule ID, check if all the required tags (`req_tags`) meet the conditions
- Find the first rule ID that matches

Leveraging Linguistics

- Find the words that match the required part of the speech tags
- Fill in the corresponding question template and return the question string

```
def sent_to_ques(sent:str)->str:
    """
    Return a question string corresponding to a sentence string using a set
of pre-written rules
    """
    doc = nlp(sent)
    pos_tags = [token.tag_ for token in doc]
    for idx, rule in enumerate(ruleset):
        if rule['id'] == 1:
            if all(key in pos_tags for key in rule['req_tags']):
                print(f"Rule id {rule['id']} matched for sentence: {sent}")
                NNP = get_pos_tag(doc, "NNP")
                NNP = str(NNP[0])
                VBZ = get_pos_tag(doc, "VBZ")
                VBZ = str(VBZ[0])
                ques = f'What {VBZ} {NNP}?'
                return(ques)
        if rule['id'] == 2:
            if all(key in pos_tags for key in rule['req_tags']): #'NNP',
'VBZ' in sentence.
                print(f"Rule id {rule['id']} matched for sentence: {sent}")
                NNP = get_pos_tag(doc, "NNP")
                NNP = str(NNP[0])
                VBZ = get_pos_tag(doc, "VBZ")
                VBZ = str(VBZ[0].lemma_)
                ques = f'What does {NNP} {VBZ}?'
                return(ques)
```

Within each rule ID match, I do something more: I drop all but the first match for each part-of-speech tag that I receive. For instance, when I query for NNP, I later pick the first element with NNP[0], convert it into a string, and drop all other matches.

While this is a perfectly good approach for simple sentences, this breaks down when you have conditional statements or complex reasoning. Let's run the preceding function for each sentence in the example text and see what questions we get:

```
for sent in doc.sents:
    print(f"The generated question is: {sent_to_ques(str(sent))}")

Rule id 1 matched for sentence: Bansoori is an Indian classical instrument.
The generated question is: What is Bansoori?
Rule id 2 matched for sentence: Tom plays Bansoori and Guitar.
The generated question is: What does Tom play?
```

This is quite good. In practice, you will need a much larger set, maybe 10-15 rulesets and corresponding templates just to have a decent coverage of *What?* questions.

Another few rulesets might be needed to cover *When*, *Who*, and *Where* type questions. For instance, *Who plays Bansoori?* is also a valid question from the second sentence that we have in the preceding code.

Question and answer generation using dependency parsing

This means PoS tagging and a rule-driven engine can have large coverage and reasonable precision with respect to the questions – but it will still be a little tedious to maintain, debug, and generalize this system.

We need a set of better tools that is less reliant on the *state* of tokens and more on the relationship between them. This will allow you to change the relationship to form a question instead. This is where dependency parsing comes in.

What is a dependency parser?

> *"A dependency parser analyzes the grammatical structure of a sentence, establishing relationships between "head" words and words which modify those heads."*
>
> - *from* `Stanford NNDEP Project`

A dependency parser helps us understand the various ways in which parts of the sentence interact or depend on each other. For instance, how is a noun modified by adjectives?

```
for token in doc:
    print(token, token.dep_)

Bansoori nsubj
is ROOT
an det
Indian amod
classical amod
instrument attr
. punct
Tom nsubj
plays ROOT
Bansoori dobj
and cc
```

```
Guitar conj
. punct
```

Some of these terms are simple enough to guess, for example, `ROOT` is where the dependency tree might begin, `nsubj` is the noun or nominal subject, and `cc` is a conjunction. However, this is still incomplete. Luckily for us, spaCy includes the nifty `explain()` function to help us interpret these:

```
for token in doc:
    print(token, token.dep_, spacy.explain(token.dep_))
```

This gives us the following explainer text:

```
Bansoori nsubj nominal subject
is ROOT None
an det determiner
Indian amod adjectival modifier
classical amod adjectival modifier
instrument attr attribute
. punct punctuation
Tom nsubj nominal subject
plays ROOT None
Bansoori dobj direct object
and cc coordinating conjunction
Guitar conj conjunct
. punct punctuation
```

This gives us a good starting point to Google away and pick up some linguistics-specific terms. For example, a *conjunct* is often used to connect two clauses, while an *attribute* is simply a way to highlight something which is a property of the nominal subject.

 Nominal subjects are usually nouns or pronouns, which, in turn, are actors (via verbs) or have properties (via attributes).

Visualizing the relationship

spaCy has a built-in tool called **displacy** for displaying simple, but clean and powerful visualizations. It offers two primary modes: named entity recognition and dependency parsing. Here, we will use the `dep`, or dependency mode:

```
displacy.render(doc, style='dep', jupyter=True)
```

Let's take the first sentence for a quick study: we can see that **instrument** is **amod**, or adjectively modified by **Indian classicial**. We pulled this phrase earlier as a noun chunk:

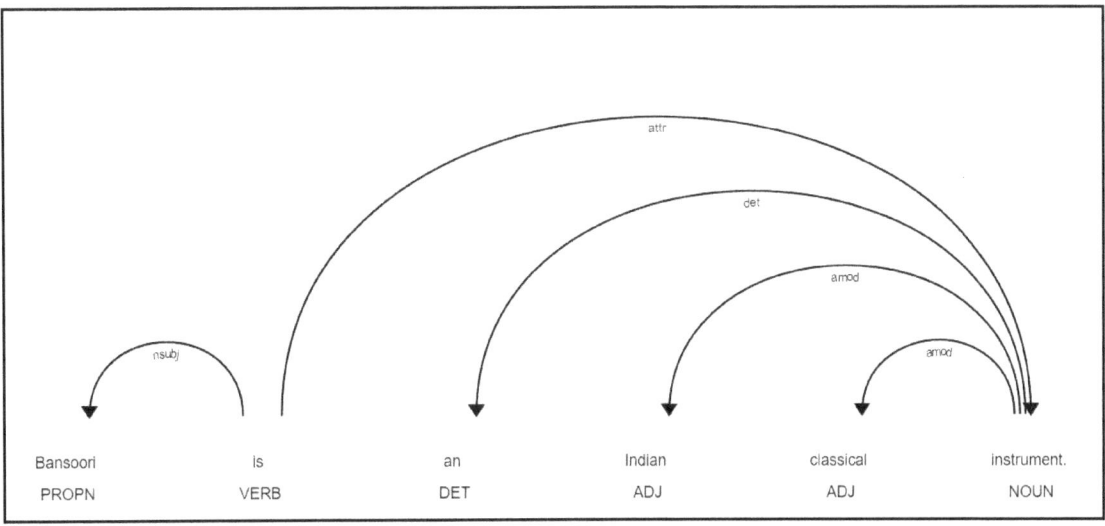

This means that when we pulled noun phrase chunks out of this sentence, spaCy must have finished dependency parsing already under the hood.

Also, notice the direction of arrows while the NOUN (instrument) is being modified by ADJ. It is the `attr` of the ROOT VERB (is).

I leave the dependency visualization of the second sentence up to you to complete:

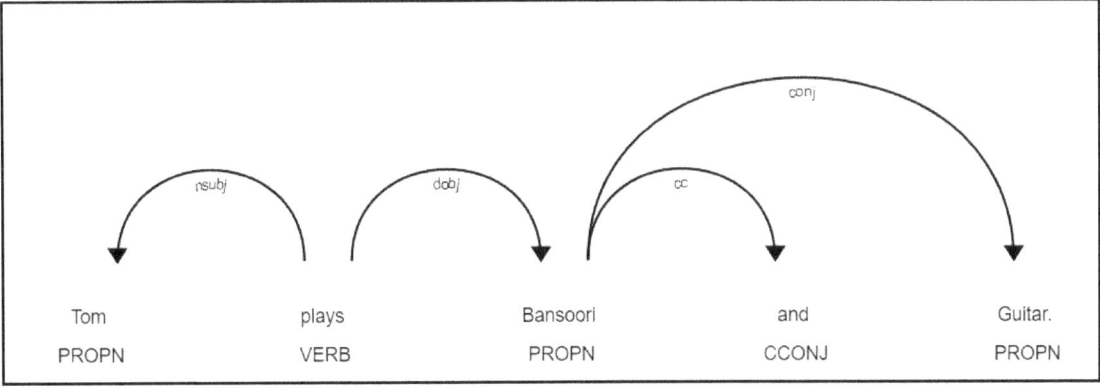

[63]

This logical tree structure of simple sentences is what we will exploit to simplify our question generation. To do this, we need two important pieces of information

- The main verb, also known as the ROOT
- The subjects on which this ROOT verb is acting

Let's write some functions to extract these dependency entities in the spaCy token format, without converting them into strings.

Introducing textacy

Alternatively, we can import them from textacy itself:

```
from textacy.spacier import utils as spacy_utils
```

Inside a Jupyter Notebook, you can see the docstring AND function implementation by using the ?? syntax inside the Jupyter Notebook itself:

```
??spacy_utils.get_main_verbs_of_sent
# Signature: spacy_utils.get_main_verbs_of_sent(sent)
# Source:
# def get_main_verbs_of_sent(sent):
#     """Return the main (non-auxiliary) verbs in a sentence."""
#     return [tok for tok in sent
#             if tok.pos == VERB and tok.dep_ not in constants.AUX_DEPS]
# File:      d:\miniconda3\envs\nlp\lib\site-packages\textacy\spacier\utils.py
# Type:      function
```

Usually, when you ask somebody a question, they are often about a piece of information, for example, *What is the capital of India?* Sometimes, they are also about a certain action, for example, *What did you do on Sunday?*

Answering *what* means that we need to find out what the verbs are acting on. This means that we need to find the subjects of the verb. Let's take a more concrete but simple example to explore this:

```
toy_sentence = 'Shivangi is an engineer'
doc = nlp(toy_sentence)
```

What are the entities in this sentence?

```
displacy.render(doc, style='ent', jupyter=True)
```

Shivangi PERSON is an engineer

 The preceding example might return ORG for the smaller en model. This is why using `en_core_web_lg` is important. It gives much better performance.

Let's try the first few lines of Berlin's Wikipedia entry:

```
displacy.render(nlp("Berlin, German pronunciation: [bɛɐ̯ˈliːn]) is the capital
and the largest city of Germany, as well as one of its 16 constituent
states. With a steadily growing population of approximately 3.7 million,
Berlin is the second most populous city proper in the European Union behind
London and the seventh most populous urban area in the European Union"),
style='ent', jupyter=True)
```

Berlin GPE , German NORP pronunciation: [bɛɐ̯ˈli n]) is the capital and the largest city of Germany GPE , as well as one CARDINAL of its 16 CARDINAL constituent states. With a steadily growing population of approximately 3.7 million MONEY , Berlin GPE is the second ORDINAL most populous city proper in the European Union ORG behind London GPE and the seventh ORDINAL most populous urban area in the European Union ORG

Let's find out the main verb in this sentence:

```
verbs = spacy_utils.get_main_verbs_of_sent(doc)
print(verbs)
>> [is]
```

And what are the nominal subjects of this verb?

```
for verb in verbs:
    print(verb, spacy_utils.get_subjects_of_verb(verb))
>> is [Shivangi]
```

You will notice that this has a reasonable overlap with the noun phrases that we pulled from our part-of-speech tagging. However, some of them are different, too:

```
print([(token, token.tag_) for token in doc])
>>[(Shivangi, 'NNP'), (is, 'VBZ'), (an, 'DT'), (engineer, 'NN')]
```

Leveraging Linguistics

 As an exercise, extend this approach to at least add *Who*, *Where*, and *When* questions as a best practice.

Leveling up – question and answer

So far, we have been trying to generate questions. But if you were trying to make an automated quiz for students, you would also need to mine the right answer.

The answer, in this case, will be simply the objects of a verb. What is an object of a verb?

> *In the sentence, "Give the book to me", "book" is the direct object of the verb "give", and "me" is the indirect object.*
>
> *– from the Cambridge English Dictionary*

Loosely, the object is the piece on which our verb acts. This is almost always the answer to our *what* question. Let's write a question to find the objects of any verb – or, we can pull it from `textacy.spacier.utils.`:

```
spacy_utils.get_objects_of_verb(verb)
>> [engineer]
```

Let's do this for all of the verbs:

```
for verb in verbs:
    print(verb, spacy_utils.get_objects_of_verb(verb))
>> is [engineer]
```

Let's look at the output of our functions from the example text. The first is the sentence itself, then the root verb, then the lemma form of that verb, followed by the subjects of the verb, and finally the objects:

```
doc = nlp(example_text)
for sentence in doc.sents:
    print(sentence, sentence.root, sentence.root.lemma_,
spacy_utils.get_subjects_of_verb(sentence.root),
spacy_utils.get_objects_of_verb(sentence.root))

>> Bansoori is an Indian classical instrument. is be [Bansoori]
[instrument]
>> Tom plays Bansoori and Guitar. plays play [Tom] [Bansoori, Guitar]
```

Let's arrange the preceding pieces of information into a neat function that we can then reuse:

```
def para_to_ques(eg_text):
    doc = nlp(eg_text)
    results = []
    for sentence in doc.sents:
        root = sentence.root
        ask_about = spacy_utils.get_subjects_of_verb(root)
        answers = spacy_utils.get_objects_of_verb(root)
        if len(ask_about) > 0 and len(answers) > 0:
            if root.lemma_ == "be":
                question = f'What {root} {ask_about[0]}?'
            else:
                question = f'What does {ask_about[0]} {root.lemma_}?'
            results.append({'question':question, 'answers':answers})
    return results
```

Let's run it on our example text and see where it goes:

```
para_to_ques(example_text)
>> [{'question': 'What is Bansoori?', 'answers': [instrument]},
>> {'question': 'What does Tom play?', 'answers': [Bansoori, Guitar]}]
```

This seems right to me. Let's run this on a larger sample of sentences. This sample has varying degrees of complexities and sentence structures:

```
large_example_text = """
Puliyogare is a South Indian dish made of rice and tamarind.
Priya writes poems. Shivangi bakes cakes. Sachin sings in the orchestra.

Osmosis is the movement of a solvent across a semipermeable membrane toward
a higher concentration of solute. In biological systems, the solvent is
typically water, but osmosis can occur in other liquids, supercritical
liquids, and even gases.
When a cell is submerged in water, the water molecules pass through the
cell membrane from an area of low solute concentration to high solute
concentration. For example, if the cell is submerged in saltwater, water
molecules move out of the cell. If a cell is submerged in freshwater, water
molecules move into the cell.

Raja-Yoga is divided into eight steps. The first is Yama. Yama is
nonviolence, truthfulness, continence, and non-receiving of any gifts.
After Yama, Raja-Yoga has Niyama. cleanliness, contentment, austerity,
study, and self - surrender to God.
The steps are Yama and Niyama.
"""
```

Let's run it on the whole large example text:

```
para_to_ques(large_example_text)

>> [{'question': 'What is Puliyogare?', 'answers': [dish]},
 {'question': 'What does Priya write?', 'answers': [poems]},
 {'question': 'What does Shivangi bake?', 'answers': [cakes]},
 {'question': 'What is Osmosis?', 'answers': [movement]},
 {'question': 'What is solvent?', 'answers': [water]},
 {'question': 'What is first?', 'answers': [Yama]},
 {'question': 'What is Yama?',
  'answers': [nonviolence, truthfulness, continence, of]},
 {'question': 'What does Yoga have?', 'answers': [Niyama]},
 {'question': 'What are steps?', 'answers': [Yama, Niyama]}]
```

Putting it together and the end

Linguistics is incredibly powerful. I have given you only a taste of its immense utility here. We looked at two motivating use cases and a lot of powerful ideas. For each use case, I have listed the related idea here:

- Redacting names:
    - Named entity recognition
- Question and answer generation:
    - Part-of-speech tagging
    - Lemmatization
    - Dependency parsing

Summary

We now have a way to generate questions and answers. What were you going to ask the user? Can you match our answers against the user's answers?

Sure, an exact match is perfect. But we should also be looking for *meaning* matches, for example, *cake* with *pastry*, or *honesty* with *truthfulness*.

We could use a synonym dictionary – but how do we extend this into sentences and documents?

In the next chapter, we will answer all of these questions using text representations.

4
Text Representations - Words to Numbers

Computers today cannot act on words or text directly. They need to be represented by meaningful number sequences. These long sequences of decimal numbers are called vectors, and this step is often referred to as the vectorization of text.

So, where are these word vectors used:

- In text classification and summarization tasks
- During similar word searches, such as synonyms
- In machine translation (for example, when translating text from English to German)
- When understanding similar texts (for example, Facebook articles)
- During question and answer sessions, and general tasks (for example, chatbots used in appointment scheduling)

Very frequently, we see word vectors used in some form of categorization task. For instance, using a machine learning or deep learning model for sentiment analysis, with the following text vectorization methods:

- TF-IDF in sklearn pipelines with logistic regression
- GLoVe by Stanford, looked up via Gensim
- fastText by Facebook using pre-trained vectors

We have already seen TF-IDF examples, and will see several more throughout this book. This chapter will instead cover the other ways in which you can vectorize your text corpus or a part of it.

In this chapter, we will learn about the following topics:

- How to vectorize a specific dataset
- How to make document embedding

Vectorizing a specific dataset

This section focuses almost exclusively on word vectors and how we can leverage the Gensim library to perform them.

Some of the questions we want to answer in this section include these:

- How do we use original embedding, such as GLoVe?
- How do we handle Out of Vocabulary words? (Hint: fastText)
- How do we train our own word2vec vectors on our own corpus?
- How do we train our own word2vec vectors?
- How do we train our own fastText vectors?
- How do we use similar words to compare both of the above?

First, let's get started with some simple imports, as follows:

```
import gensim
print(f'gensim: {gensim.__version__}')
> gensim: 3.4.0
```

Please ensure that your Gensim version is at least 3.4.0. This is a very popular package which is maintained and developed mostly by text processing experts over at RaRe Technologies. They use the same library in their own work for enterprise B2B consulting. Large parts of Gensim's internal implementations are written in Cython for speed. It natively uses multiprocessing.

Here, the caveat is that Gensim is known to make breaking API changes, so consider double-checking the API when you use the code with their documents or tutorials.

If you using a Windows machine, watch out for a warning similar to the following:

```
C:\Users\nirantk\Anaconda3\envs\fastai\lib\site-
packages\Gensim\utils.py:1197: UserWarning: detected Windows; aliasing
chunkize to chunkize_serial
  warnings.warn("detected Windows; aliasing chunkize to chunkize_serial")
```

Now, let's get started by downloading the pre-trained GloVe embedding. While we could do this manually, here we will download it using the following Python code:

```
from tqdm import tqdm
class TqdmUpTo(tqdm):
    def update_to(self, b=1, bsize=1, tsize=None):
        if tsize is not None: self.total = tsize
        self.update(b * bsize - self.n)

def get_data(url, filename):
    """
    Download data if the filename does not exist already
    Uses Tqdm to show download progress
    """
    import os
    from urllib.request import urlretrieve
    if not os.path.exists(filename):

        dirname = os.path.dirname(filename)
        if not os.path.exists(dirname):
            os.makedirs(dirname)

        with TqdmUpTo(unit='B', unit_scale=True, miniters=1,
desc=url.split('/')[-1]) as t:
            urlretrieve(url, filename, reporthook=t.update_to)
```

We will also reuse the `get_data` API to download any arbitrary files that we want to use throughout this section. We have also set up `tqdm` (Arabic for progress), which provides us with a progress bar by wrapping our `urlretrieve` iterable in it.

The following text is from tqdm's README:

> *tqdm works on any platform (Linux, Windows, Mac, FreeBSD, NetBSD, Solaris/SunOS), in any console or in a GUI, and is also friendly with IPython/Jupyter notebooks.*

> *tqdm does not require any dependencies (not even curses!), just Python and an environment supporting carriage return \r and line feed \n control characters.*

Text Representations - Words to Numbers

Right, let's finally download the embedding, shall we?

```
embedding_url = 'http://nlp.stanford.edu/data/glove.6B.zip'
get_data(embedding_url, 'data/glove.6B.zip')
```

The preceding snippet will download a large file with GLoVe word representations of 6 billion English words.

Let's quickly unzip the file using the Terminal or command-line syntax in Jupyter notebooks. You can also do this manually or by writing code, as follows:

```
# # We need to run this only once, can unzip manually unzip to the data directory too
# !unzip data/glove.6B.zip
# !mv glove.6B.300d.txt data/glove.6B.300d.txt
# !mv glove.6B.200d.txt data/glove.6B.200d.txt
# !mv glove.6B.100d.txt data/glove.6B.100d.txt
# !mv glove.6B.50d.txt data/glove.6B.50d.txt
```

Here, we have moved all of the `.txt` files back to the `data` directory. The thing to note here is in the filename, `glove.6B.50d.txt`.

`6B` stands for the 6 billion words or tokens. `50d` stands for 50 dimensions, which means that each word is represented by a sequence of 50 numbers, and in this case, that's 50 float numbers.

We'll now deviate a little to give you some context about word representations.

Word representations

The most popular names in word embedding are word2vec by Google (Mikolov) and GloVe by Stanford (Pennington, Socher, and Manning). fastText seems to be fairly popular for multilingual sub-word embeddings.

We advise that you don't use word2vec or GloVe. Instead, use fastText vectors, which are much better and from the same authors. word2vec was introduced by T. Mikolov et. al. (https://scholar.google.com/citations?user=oBu8kMMAAAAJhl=en) when he was with Google, and it performs well on word similarity and analogy tasks.

GloVe was introduced by Pennington, Socher, and Manning from Stanford in 2014 as a statistical approximation for word embedding. The word vectors are created by the matrix factorization of word-word co-occurrence matrices.

If picking between the lesser of two evils, we recommend using GloVe over word2vec. This is because GloVe outperforms word2vec in most machine learning tasks and NLP challenges in academia.

Skipping the original word2vec here, we will now look at the following topics:

- How do we use original embeddings in GLoVe?
- How do we handle out of vocabulary words? (Hint: fastText)
- How do we train our own word2vec vectors on our own corpus?

How do we use pre-trained embeddings?

We just downloaded these.

The file formats used by word2vec and GloVe are slightly different from each other. We'd like a consistent API to look up any word embedding, and we can do this by converting the embedding format. Note that there are minor differences in how word embedding is stored.

This format conversion can be done using Gensim's API called `glove2word2vec`. We will use this to convert our GloVe embedding information to the word2vec format.

So, let's get the imports out of the way and begin by setting up filenames, as follows:

```
from gensim.scripts.glove2word2vec import glove2word2vec
glove_input_file = 'data/glove.6B.300d.txt'
word2vec_output_file = 'data/glove.6B.300d.word2vec.txt'
```

We don't want to repeat this step if we have already done the conversion once. The simplest way to check this is to see if `word2vec_output_file` already exists. We run the following conversion only if the file does not exist:

```
import os
if not os.path.exists(word2vec_output_file):
    glove2word2vec(glove_input_file, word2vec_output_file)
```

The preceding snippet will create a new file in a standard that is compatible with the rest of Gensim's API stack.

KeyedVectors API

We now have to perform the simple task of loading vectors from a file. We do this using the `KeyedVectors` API in **Gensim**. The word we want to look up is the key, and the numerical representation of that word is the corresponding value.

Let's first import the API and set up the target filename as follows:

```
from gensim.models import KeyedVectors
filename = word2vec_output_file
```

We will load the entire text file into our memory, thus including the read from disk time. In most running processes, this is a one-off I/O step and is not repeated for every new data pass. This becomes our Gensim model, detailed as follows:

```
%%time
# load the Stanford GloVe model from file, this is Disk I/O and can be slow
pretrained_w2v_model =
KeyedVectors.load_word2vec_format(word2vec_output_file, binary=False)
# binary=False format for human readable text (.txt) files, and binary=True
for .bin files
```

A faster SSD should definitely speed this up by an order of magnitude.

We can do some word vector arithmetic to compose and show that this representation captures semantic meaning as well. For instance, let's repeat the following famous word vector example:

```
(king - man) + woman = ?
```

Let's now perform the mentioned arithmetic operations on the word vectors, as follows:

```
# calculate: (king - man) + woman = ?
result = pretrained_w2v_model.wv.most_similar(positive=['woman', 'king'],
negative=['man'], topn=1)
```

We did this using the `most_similar` API. Behind the scenes, Gensim has done the following for us:

1. Looked up the vectors for `woman`, `king`, and `man`
2. Added `king` and `woman`, and subtracted the vector from `man` to find a resultant vector
3. From the 6 billion tokens in this model, ranked all words by distance and found the closest words
4. Found the closest word

We also added `topn=1` to tell the API that we are only interested in the closest match. The expected output is now just one word, `'queen'`, as shown in the following snippet:

```
print(result)
> [('queen', 0.6713277101516724)]
```

Not only did we get the correct word, but also an accompanying decimal number! We will ignore that for now, but note that the number represents a notion of how close or similar the word is to the resultant vector that the API computed for us.

Let's try a few more examples, say social networks, as shown in the following snippet:

```
result = pretrained_w2v_model.most_similar(positive=['quora', 'facebook'],
negative=['linkedin'], topn=1)
print(result)
```

In this example, we are looking for a social network that is more casual than LinkedIn but more focused on learning than Facebook by adding Quora. As you can see in the following output, it looks like Twitter fits the bill perfectly:

```
[('twitter', 0.37966805696487427)]
```

We could have equally expected Reddit to fit this.

So, can we use this approach to simply explore similar words in a larger corpus? It seems so. Let's now look up words most similar to `india`, as shown in the following snippet. Notice that we are writing India in lowercase; this is because the model contains only lowercase words:

```
pretrained_w2v_model.most_similar('india')
```

It is worth mentioning that these results might be a little biased because GloVe was primarily trained on a large news corpus called Gigaword:

```
[('indian', 0.7355823516845703),
 ('pakistan', 0.7285579442977905),
 ('delhi', 0.6846907138824463),
 ('bangladesh', 0.6203191876411438),
 ('lanka', 0.609517514705658),
 ('sri', 0.6011613607406616),
 ('kashmir', 0.5746493935585022),
 ('nepal', 0.5421023368835449),
 ('pradesh', 0.5405811071395874),
 ('maharashtra', 0.518537700176239)]
```

The preceding result does make sense, keeping in mind that, in the foreign press, India is often mentioned because of its troubled relationships with its geographical neighbours, including Pakistan and Kashmir. Bangladesh, Nepal, and Sri Lanka are neighbouring countries, while Maharashtra is the home of India's business capital, Mumbai.

What is missing in both word2vec and GloVe?

Neither GloVe nor word2vec can handle words they didn't see during training. These words are called **Out of Vocabulary** (OOV), in the literature.

Evidence of this can be seen if you try to look up nouns that are not frequently used, for example an uncommon name. As you can see in the following snippet, the model throws a `not in vocabulary` error:

```
try:
    pretrained_w2v_model.wv.most_similar('nirant')
except Exception as e:
    print(e)
```

This results in the following output:

```
"word 'nirant' not in vocabulary"
```

This result is also accompanied by an API warning that sometimes states the API will change in gensim v4.0.0.

How do we handle Out Of Vocabulary words?

The authors of word2vec (Mikolov et al.) extended it to create fastText at Facebook. It works on character n-grams instead of entire words. Character n-grams are effective in languages with specific morphological properties.

We can create our own fastText embeddings, which can handle OOV tokens as well.

Getting the dataset

First, we need to download the subtitles of several TED talks from a public dataset. We will train our fastText embeddings on these as well as the word2vec embeddings for comparison, as follows:

```
ted_dataset = "https://wit3.fbk.eu/get.php?path=XML_releases/xml/ted_en-20160408.zip&filename=ted_en-20160408.zip"
get_data(ted_dataset, "data/ted_en.zip")
```

Python empowers us to access files inside a `.zip` file, which is easy to do with the `zipfile` package. Notice it is the `zipfile.zipFile` syntax that enables this.

We additionally use the `lxml` package to `parse` the XML file inside the ZIP.

Here, we manually opened the file to find the relevant `content` path and look up `text()` from it. In this case, we are interested only in the subtitles and not any accompanying metadata, as follows:

```
import zipfile
import lxml.etree
with zipfile.ZipFile('data/ted_en.zip', 'r') as z:
    doc = lxml.etree.parse(z.open('ted_en-20160408.xml', 'r'))
input_text = '\n'.join(doc.xpath('//content/text()'))
```

Let's now preview the first 500 characters of the following `input_text`:

```
input_text[:500]
> "Here are two reasons companies fail: they only do more of the same, or
they only do what's new.\nTo me the real, real solution to quality growth
is figuring out the balance between two activities: exploration and
exploitation. Both are necessary, but it can be too much of a good
thing.\nConsider Facit. I'm actually old enough to remember them. Facit was
a fantastic company. They were born deep in the Swedish forest, and they
made the best mechanical calculators in the world. Everybody used them. A"
```

Text Representations - Words to Numbers

Since we are using subtitles from TED talks, there are some fillers that are not useful. These are often words describing sounds in parentheses and the speaker's name.

Let's remove these fillers using some regex, as follows:

```
import re
# remove parenthesis
input_text_noparens = re.sub(r'\([^)]*\)', '', input_text)

# store as list of sentences
sentences_strings_ted = []
for line in input_text_noparens.split('\n'):
    m = re.match(r'^(?:(?P<precolon>[^:]{,20}):)?(?P<postcolon>.*)$', line)
    sentences_strings_ted.extend(sent for sent in m.groupdict()['postcolon'].split('.') if sent)

# store as list of lists of words
sentences_ted = []
for sent_str in sentences_strings_ted:
    tokens = re.sub(r"[^a-z0-9]+", " ", sent_str.lower()).split()
    sentences_ted.append(tokens)
```

Notice that we created `sentence_strings_ted` using the `.split('\n')` syntax on our entire corpus. Replace this with a better sentence tokenizer, such as that from spaCy or NLTK, as a reader exercise:

```
print(sentences_ted[:2])
```

Notice that each `sentences_ted` is now a list of a lists. Each element of the first list is a sentence, and each sentence is a list of tokens (words).

This is the expected structure for training text embeddings using Gensim. We will write the following code to disk for easy retrieval later:

```
import json
# with open('ted_clean_sentences.json', 'w') as fp:
#     json.dump(sentences_ted, fp)

with open('ted_clean_sentences.json', 'r') as fp:
    sentences_ted = json.load(fp)
```

I personally prefer JSON serialization over Pickle because it's slightly faster, more interoperable among languages, and, most importantly, human readable.

Let's now train both fastText and word2vec embedding over this small corpus. Although small, the corpus we are using is representative of the data sizes usually seen in practice. Large annotated text corpora are extremely rare in the industry.

Training fastText embedddings

Setting up imports is actually quite simple in the new Gensim API; just use the following code:

```
from gensim.models.fasttext import FastText
```

The next step is to feed the text and make our text embedding model, as follows:

```
fasttext_ted_model = FastText(sentences_ted, size=100, window=5,
min_count=5, workers=-1, sg=1)
 # sg = 1 denotes skipgram, else CBOW is used
```

You will probably noticed the parameters we pass to make our model. The following list explains these parameters, as explained in the Gensim documentation:

- `min_count (int, optional)`: The model ignores all words with total frequency lower than this
- `size (int, optional)`: This represents the dimensionality of word vectors
- `window (int, optional)`: This represents the maximum distance between the current and predicted word within a sentence
- `workers (int, optional)`: Use these many worker threads to train the model (this enables faster training with multicore machines; `workers=-1` means using one worker for each core available in your machine)
- `sg ({1, 0}, optional)`: This is a training algorithm, `skip-gram` if `sg=1` or CBOW

The preceding parameters are actually part of a larger list of levers that can move around to improve the quality of your text embedding. We encourage you to play around with the numbers in addition to exploring the other parameters that the Gensim API exposes.

Let's now take a quick peek at the words most similar to India in this corpus, as ranked by fastText embedding-based similarity, as follows:

```
fasttext_ted_model.wv.most_similar("india")

[('indians', 0.5911639928817749),
 ('indian', 0.5406097769737244),
 ('indiana', 0.4898717999458313),
 ('indicated', 0.4400438070297241),
 ('indicate', 0.4042605757713318),
 ('internal', 0.39166826009750366),
 ('interior', 0.3871103823184967),
 ('byproducts', 0.3752930164337158),
```

Text Representations - Words to Numbers

```
('princesses', 0.37265270948410034),
('indications', 0.369659960269928)]
```

Here, we notice that fastText has leveraged the sub-word structure, such as `ind`, `ian`, and `dian`, to rank the words. We get both `indians` and `indian` in the top 3, which is quite good. This is one of the reasons fastText is effective—even for small training text tasks.

Let's now repeat the same process using word2vec and look at the words most similar to `india` there.

Training word2vec embeddings

Importing the model is simple, simply use the following command. By now, you should have an intuitive feel of how the Gensim model's API is structured:

```
from gensim.models.word2vec import Word2Vec
```

Here, we are using an identical configuration for the word2vec model as we did for fastText. This helps to reduce bias in the comparison.

You are encouraged to compare the best fastText model to the best word2vec model with the following:

```
word2vec_ted_model = Word2Vec(sentences=sentences_ted, size=100, window=5,
min_count=5, workers=-1, sg=1)
```

Right, let's now look at the words most similar to `india`, as follows:

```
word2vec_ted_model.wv.most_similar("india")

[('cent', 0.38214215636253357),
 ('dichotomy', 0.37258434295654297),
 ('executing', 0.3550642132759094),
 ('capabilities', 0.3549191951751709),
 ('enormity', 0.3421599268913269),
 ('abbott', 0.34020164608955383),
 ('resented', 0.33033430576324463),
 ('egypt', 0.32998529076576233),
 ('reagan', 0.32638251781463623),
 ('squeezing', 0.32618749141693115)]
```

The words most similar to `india` have no tangible relation to the original word. For this particular dataset, and word2vec's training configuration, the model has not captured any semantic or syntactic information at all. This is not unusual since word2vec is meant to work on large text corpora.

fastText versus word2vec

According to the following preliminary comparison by Gensim:

fastText embeddings are significantly better than word2vec at encoding syntactic information. This is expected, since most syntactic analogies are morphology based, and the char n-gram approach of fastText takes such information into account. The original word2vec model seems to perform better on semantic tasks, since words in semantic analogies are unrelated to their char n-grams, and the added information from irrelevant char n-grams worsens the embeddings.

The source for this is: *word2vec fasttext comparison notebook* (https://github.com/RaRe-Technologies/gensim/blob/37e49971efa74310b300468a5b3cf531319c6536/docs/notebooks/Word2Vec_FastText_Comparison.ipynb).

In general, we prefer fastText because of its innate ability to handle words that it has not seen in training. It is definitely better than word2vec when working with small data (as we've shown), and is at least as good as word2vec on larger datasets.

fastText is also useful in cases where we are processing text riddled with spelling mistakes. For example, it can leverage sub-word similarity to bring `indian` and `indain` close in the embedding space.

In most downstream tasks, such as sentiment analysis or text classification, we continue to recommend GloVe over word2vec.

> The following is our recommended rule of thumb for text embedding applications: fastText > GloVe > word2vec.

Document embedding

Document embedding is often considered an underrated way of doing things. The key idea in document embedding is to compress an entire document, for example a patent or customer review, into one single vector. This vector in turn can be used for a lot of downstream tasks.

Empirical results show that document vectors outperform bag-of-words models as well as other techniques for text representation.

Among the most useful downstream tasks is the ability to cluster text. Text clustering has several uses, ranging from data exploration to online classification of incoming text in a pipeline.

In particular, we are interested in document modeling using doc2vec on a small dataset. Unlike sequence models such as RNN, where a word sequence is captured in generated sentence vectors, doc2vec sentence vectors are word order independent. This word order independence means that we can process a large number of examples quickly, but it does mean capturing less of a sentence's inherent meaning.

This section is loosely based on the doc2Vec API Tutorial from the Gensim repository.

Let's first get the imports out of the way with the following code:

```
from gensim.models.doc2vec import Doc2Vec, TaggedDocument
import gensim
from pprint import pprint
import multiprocessing
```

Now, let's pull out the talks from the doc variable we used earlier, as follows:

```
talks = doc.xpath('//content/text()')
```

To train the Doc2Vec model, each text sample needs a label or unique identifier. To do this, write a small function like the following:

```
def read_corpus(talks, tokens_only=False):
    for i, line in enumerate(talks):
        if tokens_only:
            yield gensim.utils.simple_preprocess(line)
        else:
            # For training data, add tags
            yield gensim.models.doc2vec.TaggedDocument(gensim.utils.simple_preprocess(line), [i])
```

There are a few things happening inside the preceding function; they are as follows:

- **Overloaded if condition**: This reads a test corpora and sets `tokens_only` to `True`.
- **Target Label:** This assigns an arbitrary index variable, `i`, as the target label.
- `gensim.utils.simple_preprocess`: This converts a document into a list of lowercase tokens, ignoring tokens that are too short or too long, which then yields instances of `TaggedDocument`. Since we are yielding instead of returning, this entire function is acting as a generator.

It is worth mentioning how this changes the function behavior. With a `return` in use, when a function is called it would have returned a specific object, such as `TaggedDocument` or `None` if the return is not specified. A `generator` function, on the other hand, only returns a `generator` object.

So, what do you expect the following code line to return?

```
read_corpus(talks)
```

If you guessed correctly, you'll know we expect it to return a `generator` object, as follows:

```
<generator object read_corpus at 0x0000024741DBA990>
```

The preceding object means that we can read the text corpus element by element as and when it's needed. This is exceptionally useful if a training corpus is larger than your memory size.

Understand how Python iterators and generators work. They make your code memory efficient and easy to read.

In this particular case, we have a rather small training corpus as an example, so let's read this entire corpus into working memory as a list of `TaggedDocument` objects, as follows:

```
ted_talk_docs = list(read_corpus(talks))
```

Text Representations - Words to Numbers

The `list()` statement runs over the entire corpora until the function stops yielding. Our variable `ted_talk_docs` should look something like the following:

```
ted_talk_docs[0]

TaggedDocument(words=['here', 'are', 'two', 'reasons', 'companies', 'fail',
...., 'you', 'already', 'know', 'don', 'forget', 'the', 'beauty', 'is',
'in', 'the', 'balance', 'thank', 'you', 'applause'], tags=[0])
```

Let's quickly take a look at how many cores this machine has. We will use the following code to initialize the doc2vec model:

```
cores = multiprocessing.cpu_count()
print(cores)
8
```

Let's now go and initialize our doc2vec model from Gensim.

Understanding the doc2vec API

```
model = Doc2Vec(dm=0, vector_size=100, negative=5, hs=0, min_count=2,
iter=5, workers=cores)
```

Let's quickly understand the flags we have used in the preceding code:

- `dm ({1,0}, optional)`: This defines the training algorithm; if `dm=1`, *distributed memory* (PV-DM) is used; otherwise, a distributed bag of words (PV-DBOW) is employed
- `size (int, optional)`: This is the dimensionality of feature vectors
- `window (int, optional)`: This represents the maximum distance between the current and predicted word within a sentence
- `negative (int, optional)`: If > 0, negative sampling will be used (the int for negative values specifies how many *noise words* should be drawn, which is usually between 5-20); if set to 0, no negative sampling is used
- `hs ({1,0}, optional)`: If 1, hierarchical softmax will be used for model training, and if set to 0 where the negative is non-zero, negative sampling will be used
- `iter (int, optional)`: This represents the number of iterations (epochs) over the corpus

The preceding list has been taken directly from the Gensim documentation. With that in mind, we'll now move on and explain some of the new terms introduced here, including negative sampling and hierarchical softmax.

Negative sampling

Negative sampling started out as a hack to speed up training and is now a well-accepted practice. The click point here is that in addition to training your model on what might be the correct answer, why not show it a few examples of wrong answers?

In particular, using negative sampling speeds up training by reducing the number of model updates required. Instead of updating the model for every single wrong word, we pick a small number, usually between 5 and 25, and train the model on them. So, we have reduced the number of updates from a few million, which is required for training on a large corpus, to a much smaller number. This is a classic software programming hack that works in academia too.

Hierarchical softmax

The denominator term in our usual softmax is calculated using the sum operator over a large number of words. This normalization is a very expensive operation to do at each update during training.

Instead, we can break this down into a specific sequence of calculations, which saves us from having to calculate expensive normalization over all words. This means that for each word, we use an approximation of sorts.

In practice, this approximation has worked so well that some systems use this in both training and inference time. For training, it can give a speed of up to 50x (as per Sebastian Ruder, an NLP research blogger). In my own experiments, I have seen speed gains of around 15-25x.

```
model.build_vocab(ted_talk_docs)
```

Text Representations - Words to Numbers

The API to train a doc2vec model is slightly different. We use the `build_vocab` API first to build the vocabulary from a sequence of sentences, as shown in the previous snippet. We also pass our memory variable `ted_talk_docs` here, but we could have passed our once-only generator stream from the `read_corpora` function as well.

Let's now set up some of the following sample sentences to find out whether our model learns something or not:

```
sentence_1 = 'Modern medicine has changed the way we think about
healthcare, life spans and by extension career and marriage'

sentence_2 = 'Modern medicine is not just a boon to the rich, making the
raw chemicals behind these is also pollutes the poorest neighborhoods'

sentence_3 = 'Modern medicine has changed the way we think about
healthcare, and increased life spans, delaying weddings'
```

Gensim has an interesting API that allows us to find a similarity value between two unseen documents using the model we just updated with our vocabulary, as follows:

```
model.docvecs.similarity_unseen_docs(model, sentence_1.split(),
sentence_3.split())
> -0.18353473068679

model.docvecs.similarity_unseen_docs(model, sentence_1.split(),
sentence_2.split())
> -0.08177642293252027
```

The preceding output doesn't quite make sense, does it? The sentences we wrote should have some reasonable degree of similarity that is definitely not negative.

A-ha! We forgot to train the model on our corpora. Let's do that now with the following code and then repeat the previous comparisons to see how they have changed:

```
%time model.train(ted_talk_docs, total_examples=model.corpus_count,
epochs=model.epochs)
Wall time: 6.61 s
```

On a machine with BLAS set up, this step should take less than a few seconds.

We can actually pull out raw inference vectors for any particular sentence based on the following model:

```
model.infer_vector(sentence_1.split())

array([-0.03805782,  0.09805363, -0.07234333,  0.31308332,  0.09668373,
       -0.01471598, -0.16677614, -0.08661497, -0.20852503, -0.14948   ,
```

```
           -0.20959479,   0.17605443,   0.15131783,  -0.17354141,  -0.20173495,
            0.11115499,   0.38531387,  -0.39101505,   0.12799    ,  0.0808568 ,
            0.2573657 ,   0.06932276,   0.00427534,  -0.26196653,   0.23503092,
            0.07589306,  -0.01828301,   0.38289976,  -0.04719075,  -0.19283117,
            0.1305226 ,  -0.1426582 ,  -0.05023642,  -0.11381021,   0.04444459,
           -0.04242943,   0.08780348,   0.02872207,  -0.23920575,   0.00984556,
            0.0620702 ,  -0.07004016,   0.15629964,   0.0664391 ,   0.10215732,
            0.19148728,  -0.02945088,   0.00786009,  -0.05731675,  -0.16740018,
           -0.1270729 ,   0.10185472,   0.16655563,   0.13184668,   0.18476236,
           -0.27073956,  -0.04078012,  -0.12580603,   0.02078131,   0.23821649,
            0.09743162,  -0.1095973 ,  -0.22433399,  -0.00453655,   0.29851952,
           -0.21170728,   0.1928157 ,  -0.06223159,  -0.044757  ,   0.02430432,
            0.22560015,  -0.06163954,   0.09602281,   0.09183675,  -0.0035969 ,
            0.13212039,   0.03829316,   0.02570504,  -0.10459486,   0.07317936,
            0.08702451,  -0.11364868,  -0.1518436 ,   0.04545208,   0.0309107 ,
           -0.02958601,   0.08201223,   0.26910907,  -0.19102073,   0.00368607,
           -0.02754402,   0.3168101 ,  -0.00713515,  -0.03267708,  -0.03792975,
            0.06958092,  -0.03290432,   0.03928463,  -0.10203536,   0.01584929],
          dtype=float32)
```

Here, the `infer_vector` API expects a list of tokens as an input. This should explain why we could have used `read_corpora` with `tokens_only =True` here as well.

Now that our model is trained, let's compare the following sentences again:

```
model.docvecs.similarity_unseen_docs(model, sentence_1.split(),
sentence_3.split())
0.9010817740272721

model.docvecs.similarity_unseen_docs(model, sentence_1.split(),
sentence_2.split())
0.7461058869759862
```

The new preceding output makes sense. The first and third sentences are definitely more similar than the first and second. In the spirit of exploring, let's now see how similar the second and third sentences are, as follows:

```
model.docvecs.similarity_unseen_docs(model, sentence_2.split(),
sentence_3.split())
0.8189999598358203
```

Ah, this is better. Our result is now consistent with our expectations. The similarity value is more than the first and second sentences, but less than that of the first and third, which were also almost identical in intent.

 As an anecdotal observation or heuristic, truly similar sentences have a value greater than 0.8 on the similarity scale.

We have mentioned how document or text vectors in general are a good way of exploring a data corpus. Next, we will do that to explore our corpus in a very shallow manner before leaving you with some ideas on how to continue the exploration.

Data exploration and model evaluation

One simple technique for assessing any vectorization method is to simply use the training corpus as the test corpus. Of course, we expect that we will overfit our model to the training set, but that's fine.

We can use the training corpus as a test corpus by doing the following:

- Learning a new result or *inference* vectors for each document
- Comparing the vector to all examples
- Ranking the document, sentence, and paragraph vectors according to the similarity score

Let's do this in code, as follows:

```
ranks = []
for idx in range(len(ted_talk_docs)):
    inferred_vector = model.infer_vector(ted_talk_docs[idx].words)
    sims = model.docvecs.most_similar([inferred_vector], topn=len(model.docvecs))
    rank = [docid for docid, sim in sims].index(idx)
    ranks.append(rank)
```

We have now figured out where each document placed itself in the rank. So, if the highest rank is the document itself, that's good enough. As we said, we might overfit a little on the training corpus, but it's a good sanity test nonetheless. We can find this using the frequency count via `Counter` as follows:

```
import collections
collections.Counter(ranks) # Results vary due to random seeding + very small corpus
Counter({0: 2079, 1: 2, 4: 1, 5: 2, 2: 1})
```

The `Counter` object tells us how many documents found themselves at what ranks. So, 2079 documents found themselves first (index 0), but two documents each found themselves second (index 1) and sixth (index 5) ranks. There is one document that ranked fifth (index 4) and third (index 2) respectively. All in all, this is a very good training performance, because 2079 out of 2084 documents ranked themselves first.

This helps us understand that the vectors did represent information in the document in a meaningful manner. If they did not, we would see a lot more rank dispersal.

Let's now quickly take a single document and find the most similar document to it, the least similar document, and a document that is somewhat in between in similarity. Do this with the following code:

```
doc_slice = ' '.join(ted_talk_docs[idx].words)[:500]
print(f'Document ({idx}): «{doc_slice}»\n')
print(f'SIMILAR/DISSIMILAR DOCS PER MODEL {model}')
for label, index in [('MOST', 0), ('MEDIAN', len(sims)//2), ('LEAST',
len(sims) - 1)]:
    doc_slice = ' '.join(ted_talk_docs[sims[index][0]].words)[:500]
    print(f'{label} {sims[index]}: «{doc_slice}»\n')
```

Notice how we are choosing to preview a slice of the entire document for exploration. You are free to either do this or use a small text summarization tool to create your preview on the fly instead.

The results are as follows:

```
Document (2084): «if you re here today and very happy that you are you've
all heard about how sustainable development will save us from ourselves
however when we're not at ted we're often told that real sustainability
policy agenda is just not feasible especially in large urban areas like new
york city and that because most people with decision making powers in both
the public and the private sector really don't feel as though they are in
danger the reason why here today in part is because of dog an abandoned
puppy»

SIMILAR/DISSIMILAR DOCS PER MODEL Doc2Vec(dbow,d100,n5,mc2,s0.001,t8)
 MOST (2084, 0.893369197845459): «if you are here today and very happy that
you are you've all heard about how sustainable development will save us
from ourselves however when we are not at ted we are often told that real
sustainability policy agenda is just not feasible especially in large urban
areas like new york city and that because most people with decision making
powers in both the public and the private sector really don feel as though
they re in danger the reason why here today in part is because of dog an
abandoned puppy»

MEDIAN (1823, 0.42069244384765625): «so going to talk today about
```

```
collecting stories in some unconventional ways this is picture of me from
very awkward stage in my life you might enjoy the awkwardly tight cut off
pajama bottoms with balloons anyway it was time when was mainly interested
in collecting imaginary stories so this is picture of me holding one of the
first watercolor paintings ever made and recently I've been much more
interested in collecting stories from reality so real stories and
specifically interested in collecting »

LEAST (270, 0.12334088981151581): «on june precisely at in balmy winter
afternoon in so paulo brazil typical south american winter afternoon this
kid this young man that you see celebrating here like he had scored goal
juliano pinto years old accomplished magnificent deed despite being
paralyzed and not having any sensation from mid chest to the tip of his
toes as the result of car crash six years ago that killed his brother and
produced complete spinal cord lesion that left juliano in wheelchair
juliano rose to the occasion and»
```

Summary

This chapter was more than an introduction to the Gensim API. We now know how to load pre-trained GloVe vectors, and you can use these vector representations instead of TD-IDF in any machine learning model.

We looked at why fastText vectors are often better than word2vec vectors on a small training corpus, and learned that you can use them with any ML models.

We learned how to build doc2vec models. You can now extend this doc2vec approach to build sent2vec or paragraph2vec style models as well. Ideally, paragraph2vec will change, simply because each document will be a paragraph instead.

In addition, we now know how we can quickly perform sanity checks on our doc2vec vectors without using an annotated test corpora. We did this by checking the rank dispersal metric.

5
Modern Methods for Classification

We now know how to convert text strings to numerical vectors that capture some meaning. In this chapter, we will look at how to use those with embedding. Embedding is the more frequently used term for word vectors and numerical representations.

In this chapter, we are still following the broad outline from our first, that is, text→ representations → models→ evaluation → deployment.

We will continue working with text classification as our example task. This is mainly because it's a simple task for demonstration, but we can also extend almost all of the ideas in this book to solve other problems. The main focus ahead, however, is machine learning for text classification.

To sum up, in this chapter we will be looking at the following topics:

- Sentiment analysis as a specific class and example of text classification
- Simple classifiers and how to optimize them for your datasets
- Ensemble methods

Machine learning for text

There are at least 10 to 20 machine learning techniques that are well known in the community, ranging from SVMs to several regressions and gradient boosting machines. We will select a small taste of these.

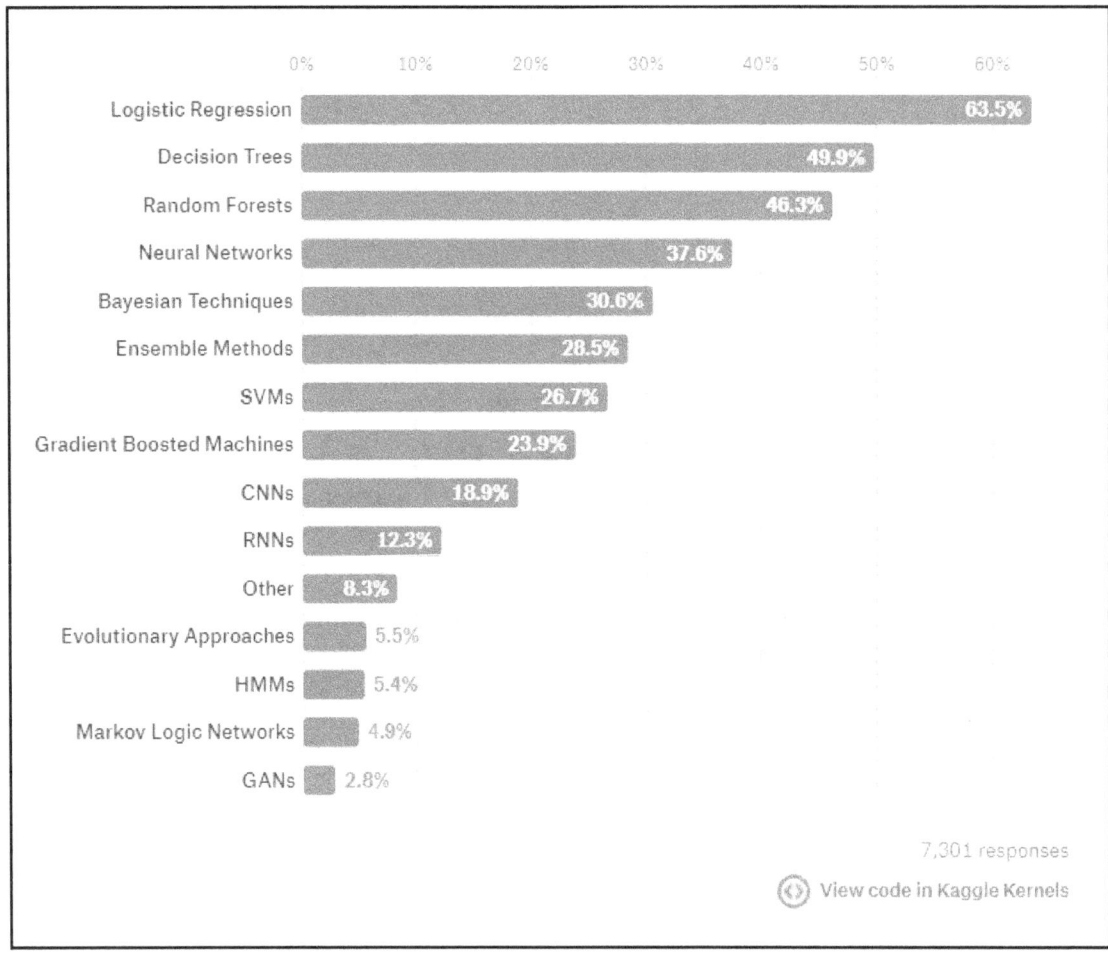

Source: https://www.kaggle.com/surveys/2017.

The preceding graph shows the most popular machine learning techniques used by Kagglers.

We met **Logistic Regression** in the first chapter while working the 20 newsgroups dataset. We will revisit **Logistic Regression** and introduce **Naive Bayes**, **SVM**, **Decision Trees**, **Random Forests**, and **XgBoost**. **XgBoost** is a popular algorithm used by several Kaggle winners to achieve award-winning results. We will use the scikit-learn and XGBoost packages in Python to see the previous example in code.

Sentiment analysis as text classification

A popular use of classifiers is in sentiment analysis. The end objective here is to determine the subjective value of a text document, which is essentially how positive or negative the content of a text document is. This is particularly handy for quickly understanding what the tone is of, say, the movie you are producing or the book you want to read.

Simple classifiers

Let's begin by simply trying a few machine learning classifiers such as Logistic Regression, Naive Bayes, and Decision Trees. We'll then move on and try the Random Forest and Extra Trees classifiers. For all of these implementations, we won't use anything except scikit-learn.

Optimizing simple classifiers

We can tweak these simple classifiers to improve their performance. For this, the most common method is to try several slightly different versions of the classifier. We do this by changing the parameters of our classifier.

We will learn how to automate this search process for the best classifier parameters using `GridSearch` and `RandomizedSearch`.

Ensemble methods

Having an ensemble of several different classifiers means we will be using a group of models. Ensembling is a very popular and easy to understand machine learning technique, and is part of almost every winning Kaggle competition.

Despite initial concerns that this process might be slow, some teams working on commercial software have begun using ensemble methods in production software as well. This is because it requires very little overhead, is easy to parallelize, and allows for a built-in fallback of using a single model.

We will look at some of the simplest ensembling techniques based on simple majority, also known as voting ensemble, and will then build using that.

In summary, this machine learning for NLP section covers simple classifiers, parameter optimization, and ensemble methods.

Getting the data

We will programmatically download the data using Python's standard inbuilt toolkit called `urlretrieve` from `urllib.request`. The following is our download-from-internet piece:

```
from pathlib import Path
import pandas as pd
import gzip
from urllib.request import urlretrieve
from tqdm import tqdm
import os
import numpy as np

class TqdmUpTo(tqdm):
    def update_to(self, b=1, bsize=1, tsize=None):
        if tsize is not None: self.total = tsize
        self.update(b * bsize - self.n)
```

If you are using the fastAI environment, all of these imports work. The second block simply sets up Tqdm for us to visualize the download progress. Let's now download the data using `urlretrieve`, as follows:

```
def get_data(url, filename):
    """
    Download data if the filename does not exist already
    Uses Tqdm to show download progress
    """
    if not os.path.exists(filename):

        dirname = os.path.dirname(filename)
        if not os.path.exists(dirname):
            os.makedirs(dirname)

        with TqdmUpTo(unit='B', unit_scale=True, miniters=1,
  desc=url.split('/')[-1]) as t:
            urlretrieve(url, filename, reporthook=t.update_to)
```

Let's download some data, as follows:

```
data_url = 'http://files.fast.ai/data/aclImdb.tgz'
get_data(data_url, 'data/imdb.tgz')
```

Let's now extract the preceding files and see what the directory contains:

```
data_path = Path(os.getcwd())/'data'/'imdb'/'aclImdb'
assert data_path.exists()
for pathroute in os.walk(data_path):
    next_path = pathroute[1]
    for stop in next_path:
        print(stop)
```

Notice that we prefer to use `Path from pathlib` over the `os.path` functionality. This make it more platform-agnostic as well as Pythonic. This really badly written utility tells us that there are at least two folders: `train` and `test`. Each of these folders, in turn, has at least three folders, as follows:

```
Test
 |- all
 |- neg
 |- pos

Train
 |- all
 |- neg
 |- pos
 |- unsup
```

The `pos` and `neg` folders contain reviews, which are positive and negative respectively. The `unsup` folder stands for unsupervised. These folders are useful for building language models, especially for deep learning, but we will not use that here. Similarly, the `all` folder is redundant because those reviews are repeated in either the `pos` or `neg` folder.

Reading data

Let's read the following data into a Pandas `DataFrame` with the appropriate labels:

```
train_path = data_path/'train'
test_path = data_path/'test'

def read_data(dir_path):
    """read data into pandas dataframe"""
    def load_dir_reviews(reviews_path):
        files_list = list(reviews_path.iterdir())
```

```
                reviews = []
                for filename in files_list:
                    f = open(filename, 'r', encoding='utf-8')
                    reviews.append(f.read())
                return pd.DataFrame({'text':reviews})
        pos_path = dir_path/'pos'
        neg_path = dir_path/'neg'
        pos_reviews, neg_reviews = load_dir_reviews(pos_path),
    load_dir_reviews(neg_path)
        pos_reviews['label'] = 1
        neg_reviews['label'] = 0
        merged = pd.concat([pos_reviews, neg_reviews])
        merged.reset_index(inplace=True)
        return merged
```

This function reads the files for a particular `train` or `test` split, both positive and negative, for the IMDb dataset. Each split is a `DataFrame` with two columns: `text` and `label`. The `label` column gives us our target value, or y, as follows:

```
train = read_data(train_path)
test = read_data(test_path)

X_train, y_train = train['text'], train['label']
X_test, y_test = test['text'], test['label']
```

We can now read the data in the corresponding `DataFrame` and then split it into the following four variables: `X_train`, `y_train`, `X_test`, and `y_test`.

Simple classifiers

In order to try some of our classifiers, let's get the basic imports out of the way, as shown in the following code. Here, we will be importing the rest of the classifiers as we need them. This ability to import things later is important for ensuring we don't import too many unnecessary components into memory:

```
from sklearn.pipeline import Pipeline
from sklearn.feature_extraction.text import CountVectorizer,
TfidfTransformer
```

Since this section is simply for illustration purposes, we will use the simplest feature extraction steps, which are as follows:

- Bag of words
- TF-IDF

We encourage you to try the code examples with better text vectorization (for example, using direct GloVe or word2vec lookups).

Logistic regression

Let's now simply replicate the simple logistic regression we did in Chapter 1, *Getting Started with Text Classification*, but on our custom dataset, as follows:

```
from sklearn.linear_model import LogisticRegression as LR
lr_clf = Pipeline([('vect', CountVectorizer()), ('tfidf',
TfidfTransformer()), ('clf',LR())])
```

As you can see in the preceding snippet, `lr_clf` becomes our classifier pipeline. We saw the pipeline in our introductory section. A pipeline allows us to queue multiple operations in one single Python object.

> We are able to call functions such as `fit`, `predict`, and `fit_transform` on our `Pipeline` objects because a pipeline automatically calls the corresponding function of the last component in the list.

```
lr_clf.fit(X=X_train, y=y_train) # note that .fit function calls are
inplace, and the Pipeline is not re-assigned
```

As mentioned earlier, we are calling the `predict` function on our pipeline. The test reviews go through under the same pre-processing steps, `CountVectorizer()` and `TfidfTransformer()`, as the reviews during training, as shown in the following snippet:

```
lr_predicted = lr_clf.predict(X_test)
```

The ease and simplicity of this process makes `Pipeline` one of the most frequently used abstractions in software-grade machine learning. However, users might prefer to execute each step independently, or build their own pipeline equivalents in some research or experimentation use cases:

```
lr_acc = sum(lr_predicted == y_test)/len(lr_predicted)
lr_acc # 0.88316
```

How do we find our model accuracy? Well, let's take a quick look at what is happening in the preceding line.

Consider that our predictions are [1, 1, 1] and the ground truth is [1, 0, 1]. The equality would return a simple list of Boolean objects, such as [True, False, True]. When we sum a Boolean list in Python, it returns the number of True cases, giving us the exact number of times our model made correct predictions.

Dividing this value by the total number of predictions made (or, equally, the number of test reviews) gives us our accuracy.

Let's write the previous two-line logic into a simple, lightweight function to calculate accuracy, as shown in the following snippet. This would prevent us from repeating the logic:

```
def imdb_acc(pipeline_clf):
    predictions = pipeline_clf.predict(X_test)
    assert len(y_test) == len(predictions)
    return sum(predictions == y_test)/len(y_test), predictions
```

Removing stop words

By simply passing a flag to the CountVectorizer step, we can remove the most common stop words. We will specify the language in which the stop words we want to remove are written. In the following case, that's english:

```
lr_clf = Pipeline([('vect', CountVectorizer(stop_words='english')),
('tfidf', TfidfTransformer()), ('clf',LR())])
lr_clf.fit(X=X_train, y=y_train)
lr_acc, lr_predictions = imdb_acc(lr_clf)
lr_acc # 0.879
```

As you can see, this is not very helpful in improving our accuracy. This would indicate that the noise added by stop words is being removed or neglected by the classifier itself.

Increasing ngram range

Let's now try to improve the information available to the classifier by including bigrams and trigrams, as follows:

```
lr_clf = Pipeline([('vect', CountVectorizer(stop_words='english',
ngram_range=(1,3))), ('tfidf', TfidfTransformer()), ('clf',LR())])
lr_clf.fit(X=X_train, y=y_train)
lr_acc, lr_predictions = imdb_acc(lr_clf)
lr_acc # 0.86596
```

Multinomial Naive Bayes

Let's initialize the classifier in a manner identical to our logistic regression classifier, as follows:

```
from sklearn.naive_bayes import MultinomialNB as MNB
mnb_clf = Pipeline([('vect', CountVectorizer()), ('clf',MNB())])
```

The previous command will measure performance on the following:

```
mnb_clf.fit(X=X_train, y=y_train)
mnb_acc, mnb_predictions = imdb_acc(mnb_clf)
mnb_acc # 0.81356
```

Adding TF-IDF

Now, let's try the preceding model with TF-IDF, as another step after bag-of-words (unigrams), as follows:

```
mnb_clf = Pipeline([('vect', CountVectorizer()), ('tfidf',
TfidfTransformer()), ('clf',MNB())])
mnb_clf.fit(X=X_train, y=y_train)
mnb_acc, mnb_predictions = imdb_acc(mnb_clf)
mnb_acc # 0.82956
```

This is better than our previous value, but let's see what else we can do to improve this further.

Removing stop words

Let's now remove the stop words for English again, by simply passing `english` to the tokenizer as follows:

```
mnb_clf = Pipeline([('vect', CountVectorizer(stop_words='english')),
('tfidf', TfidfTransformer()), ('clf',MNB())])
```

```
mnb_clf.fit(X=X_train, y=y_train)
mnb_acc, mnb_predictions = imdb_acc(mnb_clf)
mnb_acc # 0.82992
```

This helps improve performance, but only marginally. We might be better off simply keeping in the stop words for other classifiers that we try.

As a last manual experiment, let's try adding bigrams and unigrams, as we did lfor ogistic regression, as follows:

```
mnb_clf = Pipeline([('vect', CountVectorizer(stop_words='english',
ngram_range=(1,3))), ('tfidf', TfidfTransformer()), ('clf',MNB())])
mnb_clf.fit(X=X_train, y=y_train)
mnb_acc, mnb_predictions = imdb_acc(mnb_clf)
mnb_acc # 0.8572
```

This is significantly better than the previous Multinomial Naive Bayes performance, but not as good as the performance of our logistic regression classifier, which was close to achieving 88% accuracy.

Let's now try something specific to Bayesian classifiers.

Changing fit prior to false

Increasing `ngram_range` did work for us, but changing `prior` from `uniform` to fitting it (by changing `fit_prior` to `False`) did not help at all, as follows:

```
mnb_clf = Pipeline([('vect', CountVectorizer(stop_words='english',
ngram_range=(1,3))), ('tfidf', TfidfTransformer()),
('clf',MNB(fit_prior=False))])
mnb_clf.fit(X=X_train, y=y_train)
mnb_acc, mnb_predictions = imdb_acc(mnb_clf)
mnb_acc # 0.8572
```

We have now thought of each combination that might improve our performance. Note that this approach is tedious, and also error-prone because it relies too greatly on human intuition.

Support vector machines

Support vector machines (**SVM**) continue to remain a hugely popular machine learning technique, having made its way from the industry to classrooms and then back. In addition to several forms of regression, SVM is one of the techniques that forms the backbone of the multi-billion-dollar online ad targeting industry.

In academia, work such as that by T Joachim (https://www.cs.cornell.edu/people/tj/publications/joachims_98a.pdf) recommends support vector classifiers for text classification.

It's difficult to estimate whether it will be equally effective for us based on such literature, mainly due to a difference in the dataset and pre-processing steps. Let's give it a shot nevertheless:

```
from sklearn.svm import SVC
svc_clf = Pipeline([('vect', CountVectorizer()), ('tfidf',
TfidfTransformer()), ('clf',SVC())])
svc_clf.fit(X=X_train, y=y_train)
svc_acc, svc_predictions = imdb_acc(svc_clf)
print(svc_acc) # 0.6562
```

While SVM works best with linearly separable data (as we can see, our text is not linearly separable), it's still worth giving it a try for completeness.

In the previous example, SVM did not perform well, and it also took a really long time to train (~150x) when compared to other classifiers. We will not look at SVM for this particular dataset again.

Decision trees

Decision trees are simple, intuitive tools for classification and regression alike. They often resemble a flow chart of decisions when seen visually, hence the name decision tree. We will reuse our pipeline, simply using the `DecisionTreeClassifier` as our main classification technique, as follows:

```
from sklearn.tree import DecisionTreeClassifier as DTC
dtc_clf = Pipeline([('vect', CountVectorizer()), ('tfidf',
TfidfTransformer()), ('clf',DTC())])
dtc_clf.fit(X=X_train, y=y_train)
dtc_acc, dtc_predictions = imdb_acc(dtc_clf)
dtc_acc # 0.7028
```

Random forest classifier

Let's now try the first ensemble classifier. The forest in Random forest classifiers comes from the fact that each instance of this classifier consists of several decision trees. The Random in Random forests comes from the fact that each tree selects a finite number of features from all features at random, as shown in the following code:

```
from sklearn.ensemble import RandomForestClassifier as RFC
rfc_clf = Pipeline([('vect', CountVectorizer()), ('tfidf',
TfidfTransformer()), ('clf',RFC())])
rfc_clf.fit(X=X_train, y=y_train)
rfc_acc, rfc_predictions = imdb_acc(rfc_clf)
rfc_acc # 0.7226
```

Although considered to be very powerful when used in most machine learning tasks, the Random Forest approach doesn't do particularly well in our case. This is partially because of our rather crude feature extraction.

Approaches such as decision trees, RFC, and Extra trees classifiers don't do well in high-dimensional spaces such as text.

Extra trees classifier

The Extra in Extra Trees comes from the idea that it is extremely randomized. While the tree splits in a Random Forest classifier are effectively deterministic, they are randomized in the Extra Trees classifier. This changes the bias-variance trade-off in cases of high-dimensional data such as ours (where every word is effectively a dimension or classifier). The following snippet shows the classifier in action:

```
from sklearn.ensemble import ExtraTreesClassifier as XTC
xtc_clf = Pipeline([('vect', CountVectorizer()), ('tfidf',
TfidfTransformer()), ('clf',XTC())])
xtc_clf.fit(X=X_train, y=y_train)
xtc_acc, xtc_predictions = imdb_acc(xtc_clf)
xtc_acc # 0.75024
```

As you can see, this change works in our favor here, but this is not universally true. Results will vary across datasets as well as feature extraction pipelines.

Optimizing our classifiers

Let's now focus on our best performing model, logistic regression, and see if we can push its performance a little higher. The best performance for our LR-based model is an accuracy of 0.88312, as seen earlier.

We are using the phrases parameter search and hyperparameter search interchangeably here. This is done to stay consistent with deep learning vocabulary.

We want to select the best performing configuration of our pipeline. Each configuration might be different in small ways, such as when we remove stop words, bigrams, and trigrams, or similar processes. The total number of such configurations can be fairly large, and can sometimes run into the thousands. In addition to manually selecting a few combinations to try, we can try all several thousand of these combinations and evaluate them.

Of course, this process would be far too time-consuming for most small-scale experiments such as ours. In large experiments, possible space can run into the millions and take several days of computing, making it cost- and time-prohibitive.

We recommend reading a blog on hyperparameter tuning (https://www.oreilly.com/ideas/evaluating-machine-learning-models/page/5/hyperparameter-tuning) to become familiar with the vocabulary and ideas discussed here in greater detail.

Parameter tuning using RandomizedSearch

An alternative approach was proposed by Bergstra and Bengio (http://www.jmlr.org/papers/volume13/bergstra12a/bergstra12a.pdf) in 2012. They demonstrated that a random search across a large hyperparameter space is more effective than a manual approach, as we did for Multinomial Naive Bayes, and often as effective—or more so—than `GridSearch`.

How do we use it here?

Here, we will build on top of the results such as that of Bergstra and Bengio. We will break down our parameter search into the following two steps:

1. Using `RandomizedSearch`, go through a wide parameter combination space in a limited number of iterations
2. Use the results from step 1 to run `GridSearch` in a slightly narrow space

We can repeat the previous steps until we stop seeing improvements in our results, but we won't do that here. We'll leave that as an exercise for the reader. Our example is outlined in the following snippet:

```
from sklearn.model_selection import RandomizedSearchCV
param_grid = dict(clf__C=[50, 75, 85, 100],
                  vect__stop_words=['english', None],
                  vect__ngram_range = [(1, 1), (1, 3)],
                  vect__lowercase = [True, False],
                  )
```

As you can see, the `param_grid` variable defines our search space. In our pipeline, we assign names to each estimator such as `vect`, `clf`, and so on. The convention of `clf` double underscore (also called dunder) signifies that this `C` is an attribute of the `clf` object. Similarly, for `vect` we specify whether stop words are to be removed or not. As an example, `english` means removing English stop words where the list of stop words is what `scikit-learn` internally uses. You can also replace this with a command from spaCy, NLTK, or one more closely customized to your tasks.

```
random_search = RandomizedSearchCV(lr_clf, param_distributions=param_grid,
n_iter=5, scoring='accuracy', n_jobs=-1, cv=3)
random_search.fit(X_train, y_train)
print(f'Calculated cross-validation accuracy: {random_search.best_score_}')
```

The preceding code gives us a cross validation accuracy in the range of 0.87. This might vary depending on how the randomized splits are created.

```
best_random_clf = random_search.best_estimator_
best_random_clf.fit(X_train, y_train)
imdb_acc(best_random_clf) # 0.90096
```

As shown in the preceding snippet, the classifier performance improves by more than 1% by simply changing a few parameters. This is amazing progress!

Let's now take a look at what parameters we're using. In order to compare this, you need to know the default values for all of the parameters. Alternatively, we can simply look at the parameters from `param_grid` that we wrote and note the selected parameter values. For everything not in the grid, the default values are chosen and remain unchanged, as follows:

```
print(best_random_clf.steps)

[('vect', CountVectorizer(analyzer='word', binary=False,
decode_error='strict',
        dtype=<class 'numpy.int64'>, encoding='utf-8', input='content',
        lowercase=True, max_df=1.0, max_features=None, min_df=1,
        ngram_range=(1, 3), preprocessor=None, stop_words=None,
```

```
                strip_accents=None, token_pattern='(?u)\\b\\w\\w+\\b',
                tokenizer=None, vocabulary=None)),
 ('tfidf',
  TfidfTransformer(norm='l2', smooth_idf=True, sublinear_tf=False,
use_idf=True)),
 ('clf',
  LogisticRegression(C=75, class_weight=None, dual=False,
fit_intercept=True,
          intercept_scaling=1, max_iter=100, multi_class='ovr', n_jobs=1,
          penalty='l2', random_state=None, solver='liblinear',
tol=0.0001,
          verbose=0, warm_start=False))]
```

Here, we notice these things in the best classifier:

- The chosen C value in `clf` is 100
- `lowercase` is set to `False`
- Removing stop words is a bad idea
- Adding bigrams and trigrams helps

Observations like the preceding are very specific to this dataset and classifier pipeline. In my experience, however, this can and does vary widely.

Let's also avoid assuming that the values are always the best we'll get when running `RandomizedSearch` for so few iterations. The rule of thumb in this case is to run it for at least 60 iterations, and to also use a much larger `param_grid`.

Here, we used `RandomizedSearch` to understand the broad layout of parameters we want to try. We added the best values for some of those to our pipeline itself and we will continue to experiment with the values of other parameters.

We have not mentioned what the C parameter stands for or how it influences the classifier. This is definitely important when understanding and performing a manual parameter search. Changing C helps simply by trying out different values.

GridSearch

We will now run `GridSearch` for our selected parameters. Here, we are choosing to include bigrams and trigrams while running `GridSearch` over the `C` parameter of `LogisticRegression`.

Our intention here is to automate as much as possible. Instead of trying varying values in `C` during our `RandomizedSearch`, we are trading off human learning time (a few hours) with compute time (a few extra minutes). This mindset saves us both time and effort.

```
from sklearn.model_selection import GridSearchCV
param_grid = dict(clf__C=[85, 100, 125, 150])
grid_search = GridSearchCV(lr_clf, param_grid=param_grid,
scoring='accuracy', n_jobs=-1, cv=3)
grid_search.fit(X_train, y_train)
grid_search.best_estimator_.steps
```

In the preceding lines of code, we have ran the classifier over our `lr_clf` using the new, simpler `param_grid`, which works only over the `C` parameter of `LogisticRegression`.

Let's see what the steps in our best estimator are, and in particular, what the value of `C` is, as shown in the following snippet:

```
[('vect', CountVectorizer(analyzer='word', binary=False,
decode_error='strict',
        dtype=<class 'numpy.int64'>, encoding='utf-8', input='content',
        lowercase=True, max_df=1.0, max_features=None, min_df=1,
        ngram_range=(1, 3), preprocessor=None, stop_words=None,
        strip_accents=None, token_pattern='(?u)\\b\\w\\w+\\b',
        tokenizer=None, vocabulary=None)),
 ('tfidf',
  TfidfTransformer(norm='l2', smooth_idf=True, sublinear_tf=False,
use_idf=True)),
 ('clf',
  LogisticRegression(C=150, class_weight=None, dual=False,
fit_intercept=True,
        intercept_scaling=1, max_iter=100, multi_class='ovr', n_jobs=1,
        penalty='l2', random_state=None, solver='liblinear',
tol=0.0001,
        verbose=0, warm_start=False))]
```

Let's get the resulting performance directly from our object. Each of these objects has an attribute called `best_score_`. This attribute stores the best value of the metric we chose. In the following case, we have chosen accuracy:

```
print(f'Calculated cross-validation accuracy: {grid_search.best_score_}
while random_search was {random_search.best_score_}')
```

```
> Calculated cross-validation accuracy: 0.87684 while random_search was
0.87648

best_grid_clf = grid_search.best_estimator_
best_grid_clf.fit(X_train, y_train)

imdb_acc(best_grid_clf)
> (0.90208, array([1, 1, 1, ..., 0, 0, 1], dtype=int64))
```

As you can see in the preceding code, that's almost a ~3% performance gain over the non-optimized model, despite the fact we tried very few parameters to optimize.

It is worth mentioning that we can and must repeat these steps (`RandomizedSearch` and `GridSearch`) to push the model's accuracy even higher.

Ensembling models

Ensembling models is a very powerful technique for improving your model performance across a variety of machine learning tasks.

In the following section, we have quoted from the Kaggle Ensembling Guide (https://mlwave.com/kaggle-ensembling-guide/) written by MLWave.

We can explain why ensembling helps to reduce error or improve accuracy, as well as demonstrate the popular techniques on our chosen task and dataset. While each of these techniques might not result in a performance gain for us on our dataset specifically, they are still a powerful tool to have in your mental toolkit.

To ensure that you understand these techniques, we strongly urge you to try them on a few datasets.

Voting ensembles – Simple majority (aka hard voting)

The simplest ensembling technique is perhaps to take a simple majority. This works on the intuition that a single model might make an error on a particular prediction but that several different models are unlikely to make identical errors.

Let's look at an example.

Ground truth: 11011001

The numbers 1 and 0 represent a `True` and `False` prediction for an imagined binary classifier. Each digit is a single true or false prediction for different inputs.

Let's assume there are three models with only one error for this example; they are as follows:

- Model A prediction: 10011001
- Model B prediction: 11011001
- Model C prediction: 11011001

The majority votes gives us the correct answer as follows:

- Majority vote: 11011001

In the case of an even number of models, we can use a tie breaker. A tie breaker can be as simple as picking a random result, or more nuanced by picking the results with more confidence.

To try this on our dataset, we import `VotingClassifier` from scikit-learn. `VotingClassifier` does not use the pre-trained models as inputs. It will call fit on the models or classifier pipelines, and then use the predictions of all models to make the final prediction.

To counter the hype in favor of ensembles elsewhere, we can demonstrate that hard voting may hurt your accuracy performance. If someone claims that ensembling always helps, show them the following example for a more constructive discussion:

```
from sklearn.ensemble import VotingClassifier
voting_clf = VotingClassifier(estimators=[('xtc', xtc_clf), ('rfc',
rfc_clf)], voting='hard', n_jobs=-1)
voting_clf.fit(X_train, y_train)
hard_voting_acc, _ = imdb_acc(voting_clf)
hard_voting_acc # 0.71092
```

We used only two classifiers for demonstration in the preceding example: Extra Trees and Random Forest. Individually, each of these classifiers has their performance capped at an accuracy of ~74%.

In this particular example, the performance of the voting classifier is worse than both of them alone.

Voting ensembles – soft voting

Soft voting predicts the class label based on class probabilities. The sums of the predicted probabilities for each classifier areg calculated for each class (which is important in the case of multiple classes). The assigned class is then the class with the maximum probability sum or `argmax(p_sum)`.

This is recommended for an ensemble of well-calibrated classifiers, as follows:

> *Well calibrated classifiers are probabilistic classifiers for which the output of the predict_proba method can be directly interpreted as a confidence level.*
>
> *- From the Calibration Docs on sklearn* (http://scikit-learn.org/stable/modules/calibration.html)

Our code flow is identical to our hard voting classifier except that the parameter `voting` is passed as `soft`, as shown in the following snippet:

```
voting_clf = VotingClassifier(estimators=[('lr', lr_clf), ('mnb',
mnb_clf)], voting='soft', n_jobs=-1)
voting_clf.fit(X_train, y_train)
soft_voting_acc, _ = imdb_acc(voting_clf)
soft_voting_acc # 0.88216
```

Here, we can see that soft voting gives us an absolute accuracy gain of 1.62%.

Weighted classifiers

The only way for inferior models to overrule the best (expert) model is for them to collectively and confidently agree on an alternative.

To avoid this scenario, we can use a weighted majority vote—but why weighting?

Usually, we want to give a better model more weight in a vote. The simplest, but computationally inefficient, way to do this is to repeat the classifier pipelines under different names, as follows:

```
weighted_voting_clf = VotingClassifier(estimators=[('lr', lr_clf), ('lr2',
lr_clf),('rf', xtc_clf), ('mnb2', mnb_clf),('mnb', mnb_clf)],
voting='soft', n_jobs=-1)
weighted_voting_clf.fit(X_train, y_train)
```

Repeat the experiment with hard voting instead of soft voting. This will tell you how the voting strategy influences the accuracy of our ensembled classifier, as follows:

```
weighted_voting_acc, _ = imdb_acc(weighted_voting_clf)
weighted_voting_acc # 0.88092
```

Here, we can see that weighted voting gives us an absolute accuracy gain of 1.50%.

So, what have we learned so far?

- A simple majority-based voting classifier can perform worse than individual models
- Soft voting works better than hard voting
- Weighing classifiers by simply repeating classifiers can help

So far, we have been selecting classifiers seemingly at random. This is less than ideal, especially when we are building for a commercial utility where every 0.001% gain matters.

Removing correlated classifiers

Let's look at this in action by taking three simple models as an example. As you can see, the ground truth is all 1s:

```
1111111100 = 80% accuracy
1111111100 = 80% accuracy
1011111100 = 70% accuracy
```

These models are highly correlated in their predictions. When we take a majority vote, we see no improvement:

```
1111111100 = 80% accuracy
```

Now, let's compare that to the following three lower-performing but highly uncorrelated models:

```
1111111100 = 80% accuracy
0111011101 = 70% accuracy
1000101111 = 60% accuracy
```

When we ensemble this with a majority vote, we get the following result:

```
1111111101 = 90% accuracy
```

Here, we see a much higher rate of improvement than in any of our individual models. Low correlation between model predictions can lead to better performance. In practice, this is tricky to get right but is worth investigating nevertheless.

We will leave the following section as an exercise for you to try out.

As a quick hint, you will need to find the correlations among predictions of different models and select pairs that are less correlated to each other (ideally less than 0.5) and yet have a good enough performance as individual models.

```
np.corrcoef(mnb_predictions, lr_predictions)[0][1] # this is too high a correlation at 0.8442355164021454

corr_voting_clf = VotingClassifier(estimators=[('lr', lr_clf), ('mnb', mnb_clf)], voting='soft', n_jobs=-1)
corr_voting_clf.fit(X_train, y_train)
corr_acc, _ = imdb_acc(corr_voting_clf)
print(corr_acc) # 0.88216
```

So, what result do we get when we use two classifiers from the same approach?

```
np.corrcoef(dtc_predictions,xtc_predictions )[0][1] # this is looks like a low correlation # 0.3272698219282598

low_corr_voting_clf = VotingClassifier(estimators=[('dtc', dtc_clf), ('xtc', xtc_clf)], voting='soft', n_jobs=-1)
low_corr_voting_clf.fit(X_train, y_train)
low_corr_acc, _ = imdb_acc(low_corr_voting_clf)
print(low_corr_acc) # 0.70564
```

As you can see, the preceding result is not very encouraging either, but remember, this is just a hint! We encourage you to go ahead and try this task on your own and with more classifiers, including ones we have not discussed here.

Summary

In this chapter, we looked at several new ideas regarding machine learning. The intention here was to demonstrate some of the most common classifiers. We looked at how to use them with one thematic idea: translating text to a numerical representation and then feeding that to a classifier.

This chapter covered a fraction of the available possibilities. Remember, you can try anything from better feature extraction using Tfidf to tuning classifiers with `GridSearch` and `RandomizedSearch`, as well as ensembling several classifiers.

This chapter was mostly focused on pre-deep learning methods for both feature extraction and classification.

Note that deep learning methods also allow us to use a single model where the feature extraction and classification are both learned from the underlying data distribution. While a lot has been written about deep learning in computer vision, we have offered only an introduction to deep learning in natural language processing.

6
Deep Learning for NLP

n the previous chapter, we used classic machine learning techniques to build our text classifiers. In this chapter, we will replace those with deep learning techniques via the use of **recurrent neural networks** (**RNN**).

In particular, we will use a relatively simple bidirectional LSTM model. If this is new to you, keep reading – if not, please feel free to skip ahead!

The dataset attribute of the batch variable should point to the `trn` variable of the `torchtext.data.TabularData` type. This is a useful checkpoint to understand how data flow differs in training deep learning models.

Let's begin by touching upon the overhyped terms, that is, *deep* in deep learning and *neural* in deep neural networks. Before we do that, let's take a moment to explain why I use PyTorch and compare it to Tensorflow and Keras—the other popular deep learning frameworks.

I will be building the simplest possible architecture for demonstrative purposes here. Let's assume a general familiarity with RNNs and not introduce the same again.

In this chapter, we will answer the following questions:

- What is deep learning? How does it differ from what we have seen already?
- What are the key ideas in any deep learning model?
- Why PyTorch?
- How do we tokenize text and set up dataloaders with torchtext?
- What are recurrent networks, and how can we use them for text classification?

What is deep learning?

Deep learning is a subset of machine learning: a new take on learning from data that puts an emphasis on learning successive layers of increasingly meaningful representations. But what does the *deep* in deep learning mean?

> "The deep in deep learning isn't a reference to any kind of deeper understanding achieved by the approach; rather, it stands for this idea of successive layers of representations."
>
> – F. Chollet, Lead Developer of Keras

The depth of the model is indicative of how many layers of such representations we use. F Chollet suggested layered representations learning and hierarchical representations learning as better names for this. Another name could have been differentiable programming.

The term *differentiable programming*, coined by Yann LeCun, stems from the fact that what our *deep learning methods* have in common is not more layers—it's the fact that all of these models learn via some form of differential calculus – most often stochastic gradient descent.

Differences between modern machine learning methods

The modern machine learning methods that we have studied shot to being mainstream mainly in the 1990s. The binding factor among them was that they all use one layer of representations. For instance, decision trees just create one set of rules and apply them. Even if you add ensemble approaches, the *ensembling* is often shallow and only combines several ML models directly.

Here is a better-worded interpretation of these differences:

> "Modern deep learning often involves tens or even hundreds of successive layers of representations – and they're all learned automatically from exposure to training data. Meanwhile, other approaches to machine learning tend to focus on learning only one or two layers of representations of the data; hence, they're sometimes called shallow learning."
>
> – F Chollet

Let's look at the key terms behind deep learning, since this way we might come across some key ideas as well.

Understanding deep learning

In a loosely worded manner, machine learning is about mapping inputs (such as images, or *movie reviews*) to targets (such as the label cat or *positive*). The model does this by looking at (or training from) several pairs of input and targets.

Deep neural networks do this input-to-target mapping using a long sequence of simple data transformations (layers). This sequence length is referred to as the depth of the network. The entire sequence from input-to-target is referred to as a model that learns about the data. These data transformations are learned by repeated observation of examples. Let's look at how this learning happens.

Puzzle pieces

We are looking at a particular subclass of challenges where we want to learn an input-to-target mapping. This subclass is generally referred to as supervised machine learning. The word supervised denotes that we have target for each input. Unsupervised machine learning includes challenges such as trying to cluster text, where we do not have a target.

To do any supervised machine learning, we need the following in place:

- **Input Data:** Anything ranging from past stock performance to your vacation pictures
- **Target:** Examples of the expected output
- **A way to measure whether the algorithm is doing a good job:** This is necessary to determine the distance between the algorithm's current output and its expected output

The preceding components are universal to any supervised approach, be it machine learning or deep learning. Deep learning in particular has its own cast of puzzling factors:

- The model itself
- The loss function
- The optimizer

Since these actors are new to the scene, let's take a minute in understanding what they do.

Model

Each model is comprised of several layers. Each layer is a data transformation. This transformation is captured using a bunch of numbers, called layer weights. This is not a complete truth though, since most layers often have a mathematical operation associated with them, for example, convolution or an affine transform. A more precise perspective would be to say that a layer is **parameterized** by its weights. Hence, we use the terms *layer parameters* and *layer weights* interchangeably.

The state of all the layer weights together makes the model state captured in model weights. A model can have anywhere between a few thousand to a few million parameters.

Let's try to understand the notion of model **learning** in this context: learning means finding values for the weights of all layers in a network, so that the network will correctly map example inputs to their associated targets.

Note that this value set is for *all layers* in one place. This nuance is important because changing the weights of one layer can change the behavior and predictions made by the entire model.

Loss function

One of the pieces that's used to set up a machine learning task is to assess how a model is doing. The simplest answer would be to measure the notional accuracy of the model. Accuracy has few flaws, though:

- Accuracy is a proxy metric tied to validation data and not training data.
- Accuracy measures how correct we are. During training, we want to measure how far our model predicts from the target.

These differences mean that we need a different function to meet our preceding criteria. This is fulfilled by the *loss function* in the context of deep learning. This is sometimes referred to as an *objective function* as well.

"The loss function takes the predictions of the network and the true target (what you wanted the network to output) and computes a distance score, capturing how well the network has done on this specific example."
- *From Deep Learning in Python by F Chollet*

This distance measurement is called the loss score, or simply loss.

Optimizer

This loss is automatically used as a feedback signal to adjust the way the algorithm works. This adjustment step is what we call learning.

This automatic adjustment in model weights is peculiar for deep learning. Each adjustment or *update* of weights is made in a direction that will lower the loss for the current training pair (input, target).

This adjustment is the job of the optimizer, which implements what's called the backpropagation algorithm: the central algorithm in deep learning.

Optimizers and loss functions are common to all deep learning methods – even the cases where we don't have an input/target pair. All optimizers are based on differential calculus, such as **stochastic gradient descent** (**SGD**), Adam, and so on. Hence, the term *differentiable programming* is a more precise name for deep learning in my mind.

Putting it all together – the training loop

We now have a shared vocabulary. You have a notional understanding of what terms like layers, model weights, loss function, and optimizer mean. But how do they work together? How do we train them on arbitrary data? We can train them to give us the ability to recognize cat pictures or fraudulent reviews on Amazon.

Here is the rough outline of the steps that occur inside a training loop:

- Initialize:
    - The network/model weights are assigned random values, usually in the form of (-1, 1) or (0, 1).
    - The model is very far from the target. This is because it is simply executing a series of random transformations.
    - The loss is very high.
- With every example that the network processes, the following occurs:
    - The weights are adjusted a little in the correct direction
    - The loss score decreases

This is the training loop, which is repeated several times. Each pass over the entire training set is often referred to as an **epoch**. Each training set suited for deep learning should typically have thousands of examples. The models are sometimes trained for thousands of epochs, or alternatively millions of **iterations**.

In a training setup (model, optimizer, loop), the preceding loop updates the weight values that minimize the loss function. A trained network is the one with the least possible loss score on the entire training and valid data.

It's a simple mechanism that, when repeated often, just works like magic.

Kaggle – text categorization challenge

In this particular section, we are going to visit the familiar task of text classification, but with a different dataset. We are going to try to solve the `Jigsaw Toxic Comment Classification Challenge`.

Getting the data

Note that you will need to accept the terms and conditions of the competition and data usage to get this dataset.

For a direct download, you can get the train and test data from the `data tab on the challenge website`.

Alternatively, you can use the official Kaggle API (`github link`) to download the data via a Terminal or Python program as well.

In the case of both direct download and Kaggle API, you have to split your train data into smaller train and validation splits for this notebook.

You can create train and validation splits of the train data by using the `sklearn.model_selection.train_test_split` utility. Alternatively, you can download this directly from the accompanying code repository with this book.

Exploring the data

In case you have any packages missing, you can install them from the notebook itself by using the following commands:

```
# !conda install -y pandas
# !conda install -y numpy
```

Let's get the imports out of our way:

```
import pandas as pd
import numpy as np
```

Then, read the train file into a pandas DataFrame:

```
train_df = pd.read_csv("data/train.csv")
train_df.head()
```

We get the following output:

	id	comment_text	toxic	severe_toxic	obscene	threat	insult	identity_hate
0	0000997932d777bf	Explanation\r\nWhy the edits made under my use...	0	0	0	0	0	0
1	000103f0d9cfb60f	D'aww! He matches this background colour I'm s...	0	0	0	0	0	0
2	000113f07ec002fd	Hey man, I'm really not trying to edit war. It...	0	0	0	0	0	0
3	0001b41b1c6bb37e	\r\nMore\r\nI can't make any real suggestions...	0	0	0	0	0	0
4	0001d958c54c6e35	You, sir, are my hero. Any chance you remember...	0	0	0	0	0	0

Let's read the validation data and preview the same as well:

```
val_df = pd.read_csv("data/valid.csv")
val_df.head()
```

We get the following output:

	id	comment_text	toxic	severe_toxic	obscene	threat	insult	identity_hate
0	000eefc67a2c930f	Radial symmetry \r\n\r\n Several now extinct li...	0	0	0	0	0	0
1	000f35deef84dc4a	There's no need to apologize. A Wikipedia arti...	0	0	0	0	0	0
2	000ffab30195c5e1	Yes, because the mother of the child in the ca...	0	0	0	0	0	0
3	0010307a3a50a353	\r\nOk. But it will take a bit of work but I ...	0	0	0	0	0	0
4	0010833a96e1f886	== A barnstar for you! ==\r\n\r\n The Real L...	0	0	0	0	0	0

Multiple target dataset

The interesting thing about this dataset is that each comment can have multiples labels. For instance, a comment could be insulting and toxic, or it could be obscene and have `identity_hate` elements in it.

Hence, we are leveling up here by trying to predict not one label (such as positive or negative), but multiple labels in one go. For each label, we'll predict a value between 0 and 1 to indicate how likely it is to belong to that category.

This is not a probability value in the Bayesian meaning of the word, but represents the same intent.

> I'd recommend trying out the models that we saw earlier with this dataset, and re-implementing this code for our favourite IMDb dataset.

Let's preview the test dataset as well using the same idea:

```
test_df = pd.read_csv("data/test.csv")
test_df.head()
```

We get the following output:

	id	comment_text
0	00001cee341fdb12	Yo bitch Ja Rule is more succesful then you'll...
1	0000247867823ef7	== From RfC == \r\n\r\n The title is fine as i...
2	00013b17ad220c46	\r\n\r\n == Sources == \r\n\r\n * Zawe Ashto...
3	00017563c3f7919a	If you have a look back at the source, the in...
4	00017695ad8997eb	I don't anonymously edit articles at all.

This preview confirms that we have a text challenge. The focus here is on the semantic categorization of text. The test dataset does not have empty headers or columns for the target columns, but we can infer them from the train dataframe.

Why PyTorch?

PyTorch is a deep learning framework by Facebook, similar to TensorFlow by Google.

Being backed by Google, thousands of dollars have been spent on TensorFlow's marketing, development, and documentation. It also got to a stable 1.0 release almost a year ago, while PyTorch has only recently gotten to 0.4.1. This means that it's usually easier to find a TensorFlow solution to your problem and that you can copy and paste code off the internet.

On the other hand, PyTorch is programmer-friendly. It is semantically similar to NumPy and deep learning operations in one. This means that I can use the Python debugging tools that I am already familiar with.

Pythonic: TensorFlow worked like a C program in the sense that the code was all written in one session, compiled, and then executed, thereby destroying its Python flavor altogether. This has been solved by TensorFlow's Eager Execution feature release, which will soon be stable enough to use for most prototyping work.

Training Loop Visualization: Up until a while ago, TensorFlow had a good visualization tool called TensorBoard for understanding training and validation performance (and other characteristics), which was absent in PyTorch. For a long while now, tensorboardX makes TensorBoard easy to use with PyTorch.

In short, I recommend using PyTorch because it is easier to debug, more Pythonic, and more programmer-friendly.

PyTorch and torchtext

You can install the latest version of Pytorch (website) via conda or pip for your target machine. I am running this code on a Windows laptop with a GPU.

I have installed torch using `conda install pytorch cuda92 -c pytorch`.

For installing `torchtext`, I recommend using pip directly from their GitHub repository with the latest fixes instead of PyPi, which is not frequently updated. Uncomment the line when running this notebook for the first time:

```
# !pip install --upgrade git+https://github.com/pytorch/text
```

Let's set up the imports for `torch`, `torch.nn` (which is used in modeling), and `torchtext`:

```
import torch
import torch.nn as nn
import torch.nn.functional as F
import torchtext
```

If you are running this code on a machine with a GPU, leave the `use_gpu` flag set to `True`; otherwise, set it to `False`.

If you set `use_gpu=True`, we will check whether the GPU is accessible to PyTorch or not using the `torch.cuda.is_available()` utility:

```
use_gpu = True
if use_gpu:
    assert torch.cuda.is_available(), 'You either do not have a GPU or is not accessible to PyTorch'
```

Let's see how many GPU devices are available to PyTorch on this machine:

```
torch.cuda.device_count()
> 1
```

Data loaders with torchtext

Writing good data loaders is the most tedious part in most deep learning applications. This step often combines the preprocessing, text cleaning, and vectorization tasks that we saw earlier.

Additionally, it wraps our static data objects into iterators or generators. This is incredibly helpful in processing data sizes much larger than GPU memory—which is quite often the case. This is done by splitting the data so that you can make batches of batchsize samples that fit your GPU memory.

Batchsizes are often powers of 2, such as 32, 64, 512, and so on. This convention exists because it helps with vector operations on the instruction set level. Anecdotally, using a batchsize that's different from a power of 2 has not helped or hurt my processing speed.

Conventions and style

The code, iterators, and wrappers that we will be using are from `Practical Torchtext`. This is a `torchtext` tutorial that was created by Keita Kurita—one of the top five contributors to `torchtext`.

The naming conventions and style are loosely inspired from the preceding work and fastai—a deep learning framework based on PyTorch itself.

Let's begin by setting up the required variable placeholders in place:

```
from torchtext.data import Field
```

The `Field` class determines how the data is preprocessed and converted into a numeric format. The `Field` class is a fundamental `torchtext` data structure and worth looking into. The `Field` class models common text processing and sets them up for numericalization (or vectorization):

```
LABEL = Field(sequential=False, use_vocab=False)
```

Deep Learning for NLP

By default, all of the fields take in strings of words as input, and then the fields build a mapping from the words to integers later on. This mapping is called the vocab, and is effectively a one-hot encoding of the tokens.

We saw that each label in our case is already an integer marked as 0 or 1. Therefore, we will not one-hot this – we will tell the `Field` class that this is already one-hot encoded and non-sequential by setting `use_vocab=False` and `sequential=False`, respectively:

```
tokenize = lambda x: x.split()
TEXT = Field(sequential=True, tokenize=tokenize, lower=True)
```

A few things are happening here, so let's unpack it a bit:

- `lower=True`: All input is converted to lowercase.
- `sequential=True`: If `False`, no tokenization is applied.
- `tokenizer`: We defined a custom tokenize function that simply splits the string on the space. You should replace this with the spaCy tokenizer (set `tokenize="spacy"`) and see if that changes the loss curve or final model's performance.

Knowing the field

Along with the keyword arguments that we've already mentioned, the `Field` class will also allow the user to specify special tokens (`unk_token` for out-of-vocabulary unknown words, `pad_token` for padding, `eos_token` for the end of a sentence, and an optional `init_token` for the start of the sentence).

The preprocessing and postprocessing parameters accept any `torchtext.data.Pipeline` that it receives. Preprocessing is applied after tokenizing but before numericalizing. Postprocessing is applied after numericalizing, but before converting them into a Tensor.

The docstrings for the `Field` class are relatively well written, so if you need some advanced preprocessing, you should probe them for more information:

```
from torchtext.data import TabularDataset
```

`TabularDataset` is the class that we use to read `.csv`, `.tsv`, or `.json` files. You can specify the type of file that you are reading, that is, `.tsv` or `.json`, directly in the API, which is powerful and handy

At first glance, you might think that this class is a bit misplaced because a generic file I/O+processor API should be accessible directly in PyTorch and not in a package dedicated to text processing. Let's see why it is placed where it is.

`TabularData` has an interesting `fields` input parameter. For the CSV data format, `fields` is a list of tuples. Each tuple in turn is the column name and the `torchtext` variable we want to associate with it. The fields should be in the same order as the columns in the CSV or TSV file.

We have only two defined fields here: TEXT and LABEL. Therefore, each column is tagged as either one. We can simply mark the column as None if we want to ignore it completely. This is how we are tagging our columns as inputs (TEXT) and targets (LABEL) for the model to learn.

This tight coupling of the fields parameter with `TabularData` is why this is part of `torchtext` and not PyTorch:

```
tv_datafields = [("id", None), # we won't be needing the id, so we pass in
None as the field
                 ("comment_text", TEXT), ("toxic", LABEL),
                 ("severe_toxic", LABEL), ("threat", LABEL),
                 ("obscene", LABEL), ("insult", LABEL),
                 ("identity_hate", LABEL)]
```

This defines our list of inputs. I have done this manually here, but you could also do this with code by reading the column headers from `train_df` and assigning them TEXT or LABEL accordingly.

As a reminder, we will have to define another fields list for our test data because it has a different header. It has no LABEL fields.

`TabularDataset` supports two APIs: `split` and `splits`. We will use the one with the extra s, `splits`. The splits API is simple:

- `path`: This is the prefix of filenames
- `train`, `validation`: These are filenames of the corresponding dataset
- `format`: Either `.csv`, `.tsv`, or `.json`, as stated earlier; this is set to `.csv` here
- `skip_header`: This is set to `True` if your `.csv` file has column titles in it, as does ours
- `fields`: We pass the list of fields we just set up previously:

```
trn, vld = TabularDataset.splits(
     path="data", # the root directory where the data lies
```

```
            train='train.csv', validation="valid.csv",
            format='csv',
            skip_header=True, # make sure to pass this to ensure header doesn't
get proceesed as data!
            fields=tv_datafields)
```

Let's repeat the same for test data now. We drop the `id` column again and set `comment_text` to be our label:

```
tst_datafields = [("id", None), # we won't be needing the id, so we pass in
None as the field
                  ("comment_text", TEXT)
                  ]
```

We pass the entire relative file path directly into the path, instead of using the `path` and `test` variable combination here. We used the `path` and `train` combination when setting up the `trn` and `vld` variables.

As a note, these filenames are consistent with what Keita used in the `torchtext` tutorial:

```
tst = TabularDataset(
        path="data/test.csv", # the file path
        format='csv',
        skip_header=True, # if your csv header has a header, make sure to
pass this to ensure it doesn't get proceesed as data!
        fields=tst_datafields)
```

Exploring the dataset objects

Let's look at the dataset objects, that is, `trn`, `vld`, and `tst`:

```
trn, vld, tst

> (<torchtext.data.dataset.TabularDataset at 0x1d6c86f1320>,
 <torchtext.data.dataset.TabularDataset at 0x1d6c86f1908>,
 <torchtext.data.dataset.TabularDataset at 0x1d6c86f16d8>)
```

They are all objects from the same class. Our dataset objects can be indexed and iterated over like normal lists, so let's see what the first element looks like:

```
trn[0], vld[0], tst[0]
> (<torchtext.data.example.Example at 0x1d6c86f1940>,
 <torchtext.data.example.Example at 0x1d6c86fed30>,
 <torchtext.data.example.Example at 0x1d6c86fecc0>)
```

All our elements are, in turn, objects of the `example.Example` class. Each example stores each column as an attribute. But where did our text and labels go?

```
trn[0].__dict__.keys()
> dict_keys(['comment_text', 'toxic', 'severe_toxic', 'threat', 'obscene',
'insult', 'identity_hate']
```

The `Example` object bundles the attributes of a single data point together. Our `comment_text` and the `labels` are now part of the dictionary that makes up each of these example objects. We found all of them by calling `__dict__.keys()` on an `example.Example` object:

```
trn[0].__dict__['comment_text'][:5]
> ['explanation', 'why', 'the', 'edits', 'made']
```

The text has already been tokenized for us, but has not yet been vectorized or numericalized. We will use one-hot encoding for all the tokens that exist in our training corpus. This will convert our words into integers.

We can do this by calling the `build_vocab` attribute of our `TEXT` field:

```
TEXT.build_vocab(trn)
```

This statement processes the entire train data – in particular, the `comment_text` field. The words are registered in the vocabulary.

To handle the vocabulary, `torchtext` has its own class. The `Vocab` class can also take options such as `max_size` and `min_freq` that can let us know the number of words present in the vocabulary or how many times a word has to appear to be registered in the vocabulary.

Words that are not included in the vocabulary will be converted into `<unk>`, a token meaning for *unknown*. Words that occur that are too rare are also assigned the `<unk>` token for ease of processing. This can hurt or help the model's performance, depending on which and how many words we lose to the `<unk>` token:

```
TEXT.vocab
> <torchtext.vocab.Vocab at 0x1d6c65615c0>
```

Deep Learning for NLP

The TEXT field now has a vocab attribute that is a specific instance of the Vocab class. We can use this in turn to look up the attributes of the vocab object. For instance, we can find the frequency of any word in the training corpus. The TEXT.vocab.freqs object is actually an object of type collections.Counter:

```
type(TEXT.vocab.freqs)
> collections.Counter
```

This means that it will support all functions, including the most_common API to sort the words by frequency and find the top k most frequently occurring words for us. Let's take a look at them:

```
TEXT.vocab.freqs.most_common(5)
> [('the', 78), ('to', 41), ('you', 33), ('of', 30), ('and', 26)]
```

The Vocab class holds a mapping from word to id in its stoi attribute and a reverse mapping in its itos attribute. Let's look at these attributes:

```
type(TEX
T.vocab.itos), type(TEXT.vocab.stoi), len(TEXT.vocab.itos), len(TEXT.vocab.stoi.keys())
> (list, collections.defaultdict, 784, 784)
```

itos, or integer to string mapping, is a list of words. The index of each word in the list is its integer mapping. For instance, the 7-indexed word would be *and* because its integer mapping is 7.

stoi, or string to integer mapping, is a dictionary of words. Each key is a word in the training corpus, with the value being an integer. For instance, the word "and" might have an integer mapping that can be looked up in this dictionary in O(1) time.

Note that this convention automatically handles the off-by-one problem caused by zero indexing in Python:

```
TEXT.vocab.stoi['and'], TEXT.vocab.itos[7]
> (7, 'and')
```

Iterators

torchtext has renamed and extended the DataLoader objects from PyTorch and torchvision. In essence, it does the same three jobs:

- Batching the data
- Shuffling the data
- Loading the data in parallel using multiprocessing workers

This batch loading of data enables us to process a dataset that's much larger than the GPU RAM. Iterators extend and specialize the DataLoader for NLP/text processing applications.

We will use both Iterator and its cousin, BucketIterator, here:

```
from torchtext.data import Iterator, BucketIterator
```

BucketIterator

BucketIterator automatically shuffles and buckets the input sequences into sequences of similar length.

To enable batch processing, we need the input sequences in a batch that's of identical length. This is done by padding the smaller input sequences to the length of the longest sequence in batch. Check out the following code:

```
[ [3, 15, 2, 7],
  [4, 1],
  [5, 5, 6, 8, 1] ]
```

This will need to be padded to become the following:

```
[ [3, 15, 2, 7, 0],
  [4, 1, 0, 0, 0],
  [5, 5, 6, 8, 1] ]
```

Additionally, the padding operation is most efficient when the sequences are of similar lengths. The BucketIterator does all of this behind the scenes. This is what makes it an extremely powerful abstraction for text processing.

We want the bucket sorting to be based on the lengths of the comment_text field, so we pass that in as a keyword argument.

Let's go ahead and initialize the iterators for the train and validation data:

```
train_iter, val_iter = BucketIterator.splits(
        (trn, vld), # we pass in the datasets we want the iterator to draw data from
        batch_sizes=(32, 32),
        sort_key=lambda x: len(x.comment_text), # the BucketIterator needs to be told what function it should use to group the data.
        sort_within_batch=False,
        repeat=False # we pass repeat=False because we want to wrap this Iterator layer.
)
```

Let's take a quick glance at the parameters we passed to this function:

- batch_size: We use a small batch size of 32 for both train and validation. This is because I am using a GTX 1060 with only 3 GB of memory.
- sort_key: BucketIterator is told to use the number of tokens in the comment_text as the key to sort in any example.
- sort_within_batch: When set to True, this sorts the data within each minibatch in decreasing order, according to the sort_key.
- repeat: When set to True, it allows us to loop over and see a previously seen sample again. We set it to False here because we are repeating using an abstraction that we will write in a minute.

In the meanwhile, let's take a minute to explore the new variable that we just made:

```
train_iter

> <torchtext.data.iterator.BucketIterator at 0x1d6c8776518>

batch = next(train_iter.__iter__())
batch

> [torchtext.data.batch.Batch of size 25]
        [.comment_text]:[torch.LongTensor of size 494x25]
        [.toxic]:[torch.LongTensor of size 25]
        [.severe_toxic]:[torch.LongTensor of size 25]
        [.threat]:[torch.LongTensor of size 25]
        [.obscene]:[torch.LongTensor of size 25]
        [.insult]:[torch.LongTensor of size 25]
        [.identity_hate]:[torch.LongTensor of size 25]
```

Now, all that each batch has is torch tensors of exactly the same size (the size is the length of the vector of the vector of the vector of the vector of the vector of the vector of the vector here). These tensors have not been moved to GPU yet, but that's fine.

`batch` is actually a wrapper over the already familiar example object that we have seen. It bundles all the attributes related to the batch in one variable dict:

```
batch.__dict__.keys()
> dict_keys(['batch_size', 'dataset', 'fields', 'comment_text', 'toxic',
'severe_toxic', 'threat', 'obscene', 'insult', 'identity_hate'])
```

If our preceding understanding is correct, and we know how Python's object passing works, the dataset attribute of the batch variable should point to the `trn` variable of the `torchtext.data.TabularData` type. Let's check for this:

```
batch.__dict__['dataset'], trn, batch.__dict__['dataset']==trn
```

Aha! We got this right.

For the test iterator, since we don't need shuffling, we will use the plain `torchtext Iterator`:

```
test_iter = Iterator(tst, batch_size=64, sort=False,
sort_within_batch=False, repeat=False)
```

Let's take a look at this iterator, too:

```
next(test_iter.__iter__())
> [torchtext.data.batch.Batch of size 33]
    [.comment_text]:[torch.LongTensor of size 158x33]
```

The sequence length of 33 here is different from the input's 25. That's fine. We can see that this is also a torch tensor now.

Next, let's write a wrapper over the batch objects.

BatchWrapper

Before we delve into `BatchWrapper`, let me tell you what the problem with batch objects is. Our batch iterator returns a custom datatype, `torchtext.data.Batch`. This has a similar to multiple `example.Example`. This returns with a batch of data from each field as attributes. This custom datatype makes code reuse difficult since, each time the column names change, we need to modify the code. This also makes `torchtext` hard to use with other libraries such as torchsample and fastai.

So, how do we solve this?

We will convert the batch into a tuple in the form (x, y). x is the input to the model and y is the target – or, more conventionally, x is the independent variable while y is the dependent variable. One way to think about this is that the model will learn the function mapping from x to y.

BatchWrapper helps us reuse the modeling, training, and other code functions across datasets:

```
class BatchWrapper:
  def __init__(self, dl, x_var, y_vars):
      self.dl, self.x_var, self.y_vars = dl, x_var, y_vars # we pass in the list of attributes for x and y

  def __iter__(self):
      for batch in self.dl:
          x = getattr(batch, self.x_var) # we assume only one input in this wrapper
          if self.y_vars is not None:
              # we will concatenate y into a single tensor
              y = torch.cat([getattr(batch, feat).unsqueeze(1) for feat in self.y_vars], dim=1).float()
                  else: y = torch.zeros((1)) if use_gpu: yield (x.cuda(), y.cuda()) else: yield (x, y)

    def __len__(self): return len(self.dl)
```

The `BatchWrapper` class accepts the iterator variable itself, the variable x name, and the variable y name during initialization. It yields tensor x and y. The x and y values are looked up from the `batch` in `self.dl` using `getattr`.

If GPU is available, this class moves these tensors to the GPU as well with `x.cuda()` and `y.cuda()`, making it ready for consumption by the model.

Let's quickly wrap our `train`, `val`, and `test iter` objects using this new class:

```
train_dl = BatchWrapper(train_iter, "comment_text", ["toxic", "severe_toxic", "obscene", "threat", "insult", "identity_hate"])

valid_dl = BatchWrapper(val_iter, "comment_text", ["toxic", "severe_toxic", "obscene", "threat", "insult", "identity_hate"])

test_dl = BatchWrapper(test_iter, "comment_text", None)
```

This returns the simplest iterator, ready for model processing. Note that, in this particular case, the tensor has a "device" attribute set to cuda:0. Let's preview this:

```
next(train_dl.__iter__())

> (tensor([[ 453,     63,     15,   ...,    454,    660,    778],
          [ 523,      4,    601,   ...,     78,     11,    650],
          ...,
          [   1,      1,      1,   ...,      1,      1,      1],
          [   1,      1,      1,   ...,      1,      1,      1]], device='cuda:0'),
   tensor([[ 0.,    0.,    0.,    0.,    0.,    0.],
          [ 0.,    0.,    0.,    0.,    0.,    0.],
          ...,
          [ 0.,    0.,    0.,    0.,    0.,    0.],
          [ 0.,    0.,    0.,    0.,    0.,    0.]], device='cuda:0'))
```

Training a text classifier

We are now ready for training our text classifier model. Let's start with something simple: we are going to consider this model to be a black box for now.

Model architecture is better explained by other sources, including several YouTube videos such as those by CS224n at Stanford (http://web.stanford.edu/class/cs224n/). I suggest that you explore and connect it with the know-how that you already have:

```
class SimpleLSTMBaseline(nn.Module):
    def __init__(self, hidden_dim, emb_dim=300,
                 spatial_dropout=0.05, recurrent_dropout=0.1, num_linear=2):
        super().__init__() # don't forget to call this!
        self.embedding = nn.Embedding(len(TEXT.vocab), emb_dim)
        self.encoder = nn.LSTM(emb_dim, hidden_dim, num_layers=num_linear, dropout=recurrent_dropout)
        self.linear_layers = []
        for _ in range(num_linear - 1):
            self.linear_layers.append(nn.Linear(hidden_dim, hidden_dim))
        self.linear_layers = nn.ModuleList(self.linear_layers)
        self.predictor = nn.Linear(hidden_dim, 6)
    def forward(self, seq):
        hdn, _ = self.encoder(self.embedding(seq))
        feature = hdn[-1, :, :]
        for layer in self.linear_layers:
            feature = layer(feature)
        preds = self.predictor(feature)
        return preds
```

All PyTorch models inherit from `torch.nn.Module`. They must all implement the `forward` function, which is executed when the model makes a prediction. The corresponding `backward` function for training is auto-computed.

Initializing the model

Any Pytorch model is instantiated like a Python object. Unlike TensorFlow, there is no strict notion of a session object inside which the code is compiled and then run. The model class is as we have written previously.

The `init` function of the preceding class accepts a few parameters:

- `hidden_dim`: These are hidden layer dimensions, that is, the vector length of the hidden layers
- `emb_dim=300`: This is an embedding dimension, that is, the vector length of the first input *step* to the LSTM
- `num_linear=2`: The other two dropout parameters:
    - `spatial_dropout=0.05`
    - `recurrent_dropout=0.1`

Both dropout parameters act as regularizers. They help prevent the model from overfitting, that is, the state where the model ends up learning the samples in the training set instead of the more generic pattern that can be used to make predictions.

One way to think about the differences between the dropouts is that one of them acts on the input itself. The other acts during backpropagation or the weight update step, as mentioned earlier:

```
em_sz = 300
nh = 500
model = SimpleLSTMBaseline(nh, emb_dim=em_sz)
print(model)

SimpleLSTMBaseline(
  (embedding): Embedding(784, 300)
  (encoder): LSTM(300, 500, num_layers=2, dropout=0.1)
  (linear_layers): ModuleList(
    (0): Linear(in_features=500, out_features=500, bias=True)
  )
  (predictor): Linear(in_features=500, out_features=6, bias=True)
)
```

We can print any PyTorch model to look at the architecture of the class. It is computed from the forward function implementation, which is exactly what we'd expect. This is really helpful when debugging the model.

Let's write a small utility function to calculate the size of any PyTorch model. By size, we mean the number of model parameters that can be updated during training to learn the input-to-target mapping.

While this function is implemented in Keras, it's simple enough to write it again:

```
def model_size(model: torch.nn)->int:
    """
    Calculates the number of trainable parameters in any model
    Returns:
        params (int): the total count of all model weights
    """
    model_parameters = filter(lambda p: p.requires_grad, model.parameters())
#     model_parameters = model.parameters()
    params = sum([np.prod(p.size()) for p in model_parameters])
    return params

print(f'{model_size(model)/10**6} million parameters')
> 4.096706 million parameters
```

We can see that even our simple baseline model has more than 4 million parameters. In comparison, a typical decision tree might only have a few hundred decision splits, maximum.

Next, we will move the model weights to the GPU using the familiar .cuda() syntax:

```
if use_gpu:
    model = model.cuda()
```

Putting the pieces together again

These are the pieces which we looked at, let's quickly summarize them:

- **Loss function**: Binary cross entropy with Logit loss. It serves as the quality metric of how far the predictions are from the ground truth.
    - **Optimizer**: We use the Adam optimizer with default parameters, set with a learning rate of 1e-2 or 0.01:

This is how we would see these 2 components in PyTorch:

```
from torch import optim
opt = optim.Adam(model.parameters(), lr=1e-2)
loss_func = nn.BCEWithLogitsLoss().cuda()
```

We call set the number of epochs for which the model has to be trained here:

```
epochs = 3
```

This is set to a very small value because this entire notebook, model, and training loop is just for demonstrative purposes.

Training loop

The training loop is logically split into two sections: `model.train()` and `model.eval()`. Note the placement of the following lines of code:

```
from tqdm import tqdm
for epoch in range(1, epochs + 1):
    running_loss = 0.0
    running_corrects = 0
    model.train() # turn on training mode
    for x, y in tqdm(train_dl): # thanks to our wrapper, we can intuitively iterate over our data!
        opt.zero_grad()
        preds = model(x)
        loss = loss_func(preds, y)
        loss.backward()
        opt.step()
        running_loss += loss.item() * x.size(0)
    epoch_loss = running_loss / len(trn)
    # calculate the validation loss for this epoch
    val_loss = 0.0
    model.eval() # turn on evaluation mode
    for x, y in valid_dl:
        preds = model(x)
        loss = loss_func(preds, y)
        val_loss += loss.item() * x.size(0)

    val_loss /= len(vld)
    print('Epoch: {}, Training Loss: {:.4f}, Validation Loss: {:.4f}'.format(epoch, epoch_loss, val_loss))
```

The first half is the actual learning loop. This is the sequence of steps inside the loop:

1. Set the optimizer's gradient to zero
2. Make model predictions on this training batch in `preds`
3. Find the loss using `loss_func`
4. Update the model weights using `loss.backward()`
5. Update the optimizer state using `opt.step()`

The entire back propagation hassle is handled in one line of code:

```
loss.backward()
```

This level of abstraction that exposes the model's internals without worrying about the differential calculus aspects is why frameworks such as PyTorch are so convenient and useful.

The second loop is the evaluation loop. This is run on the validation split of the data. We set the model to *eval* mode, which locks the model weights. The weights will not be updated by accident as long as `model.eval()` is not set back to `model.train()`.

The only two things we do inside this second loop are simple:

- Make predictions on the validation split
- Calculate the loss on this split

The aggregate loss from all validation batches is then printed at the end of every epoch, along with running training loss.

One training loop will look something like the following:

```
100%|████████████████████████████████████| 1/1 [00:00<00:00, 2.34it/s]
Epoch: 1, Training Loss: 13.5037, Validation Loss: 4.6498
100%|████████████████████████████████████| 1/1 [00:00<00:00, 4.58it/s]
Epoch: 2, Training Loss: 7.8243, Validation Loss: 24.5401
100%|████████████████████████████████████| 1/1 [00:00<00:00, 3.35it/s]
Epoch: 3, Training Loss: 57.4577, Validation Loss: 4.0107
```

We can see that the training loop ends with a low validation loss but a high training loss. This could be indicative of something wrong with either the model or the train and valid data splits. There is no easy way to debug this.

The good way forward is usually to train the model for a few more epochs until no further change in either loss is observed.

Prediction mode

Let's use the model we trained to make some predictions on the test data:

```
test_preds = []
model.eval()
for x, y in tqdm(test_dl):
    preds = model(x)
    # if you're data is on the GPU, you need to move the data back to the cpu
    preds = preds.data.cpu().numpy()
    # the actual outputs of the model are logits, so we need to pass these values to the sigmoid function
    preds = 1 / (1 + np.exp(-preds))
    test_preds.append(preds)
test_preds = np.hstack(test_preds)
```

The entire loop is now in eval mode, which we use to lock the model weights. Alternatively, we could have set `model.train(False)` as well.

We iteratively take batchsize samples from the test iterator, make predictions, and append them to a list. At the end, we stack them.

Converting predictions into a pandas DataFrame

This helps us convert the predictions into a more interpretable format. Let's read the test dataframe and insert the predictions in the correct columns:

```
test_df = pd.read_csv("data/test.csv")
for i, col in enumerate(["toxic", "severe_toxic", "obscene", "threat", "insult", "identity_hate"]):
    test_df[col] = test_preds[:, i]
```

Now, we can preview a few of the rows of the DataFrame:

```
test_df.head(3)
```

We get the following output:

	id	comment_text	toxic	severe_toxic	obscene	threat	insult	identity_hate
0	00001cee341fdb12	Yo bitch Ja Rule is more succesful then you'll...	0.629146	0.116721	0.438606	0.156848	0.139696	0.388736
1	0000247867823ef7	== From RfC == \r\n\r\n The title is fine as i...	0.629146	0.116721	0.438606	0.156848	0.139696	0.388736
2	00013b17ad220c46	"\r\n\r\n == Sources == \r\n\r\n *. Zawe Ashto...	0.629146	0.116721	0.438606	0.156848	0.139696	0.388736

Summary

This was our first brush with deep learning for NLP. This was very a thorough introduction to `torchtext` and how we can leverage it with Pytorch. We also got a very broad view of deep learning as a puzzle of only two or three broad pieces: the model, the optimizer, and the loss functions. This is true irrespective of what framework or dataset you use.

We did skimp a bit on the model architecture explanation in the interest of keeping this short. We will avoid using concepts that have not been explained here in other sections.

When we are working with modern ensembling methods, we don't always know how a particular prediction is being made. That's a black box to us, in the same sense that all deep learning model predictions are a black box.

In the next chapter, we will look at some tools and techniques that will help us look into these boxes – at least a little bit more.

7
Building your Own Chatbot

Chatbots, better referred to as conversation software, are amazing tools for a lot of businesses. They help businesses serve their client's server 24/7 without increasing effort, with consistent quality, and the built-in option to defer to a human when bots are not enough.

They are a great example of where technology and AI has come together to improve the impact of human effort.

They range from voice-based solutions such as Alexa, to text-based Intercom chat boxes, to menu-based navigation in Uber.

A common misconception is that building chatbots needs large teams and a lot of machine learning expertise, though this is true if you are trying to build a *generic* chatbot platform like Microsoft or Facebook (or even Luis, Wit.ai, and so on).

In this chapter, we will cover the following topics:

- Why build a chatbot?
- Figuring out the right user intent
- Bot responses

Why chatbots as a learning example?

So far, we have built an application for every NLP topic that we have seen:

- Text cleaning using grammar and vocabulary insights
- Linguistics (and statistical parsers), to mine questions from text
- Entity recognition for information extraction
- Supervised text classification using both machine learning and deep learning
- Text similarity using text-based vectors such as GloVe/word2vec

We will now combine all of them into a much more complicated setup and write our own chatbot from scratch. But, before you build anything from scratch, you should ask why.

Why build a chatbot?

A related questions is why should we build our own chatbots? **Why can't I use FB/MSFT/some other cloud service?**

Perhaps, a better question to ask is *when* to build on your own? These are the factors to keep in mind when making this decision:

Privacy and competition: As a business, is it a good idea to share information about your users with Facebook or Microsoft? Or even a smaller company?

Cost and constraints: Your funky cloud limits your design choices that are made by a particular intelligence provider to those that are made by the likes of Google or Facebook. Additionally, you are now paying for each HTTP call you make, which is slower than running code locally.

Freedom to customize and extend: You can develop a solution that performs better for you! You don't have to cure world hunger –just keep shipping an everi-ncreasing business value via quality software. If you are at a big company, you have all the more reason to invest in extendible software.

Quick code means word vectors and heuristics

For the sake of simplicity, we will assume that our bot does not need to remember the context of any question. Therefore it sees input, responds to it, and is done. No links are established with the previous input.

Let's start by simply loading the word vectors using `gensim`:

```
import numpy as np
import gensim
print(f"Gensim version: {gensim.__version__}")

from tqdm import tqdm
class TqdmUpTo(tqdm):
    def update_to(self, b=1, bsize=1, tsize=None):
```

```
            if tsize is not None: self.total = tsize
            self.update(b * bsize - self.n)

    def get_data(url, filename):
        """
        Download data if the filename does not exist already
        Uses Tqdm to show download progress
        """
        import os
        from urllib.request import urlretrieve
        if not os.path.exists(filename):

            dirname = os.path.dirname(filename)
            if not os.path.exists(dirname):
                os.makedirs(dirname)

            with TqdmUpTo(unit='B', unit_scale=True, miniters=1,
    desc=url.split('/')[-1]) as t:
                urlretrieve(url, filename, reporthook=t.update_to)
        else:
            print("File already exists, please remove if you wish to download
    again")

    embedding_url = 'http://nlp.stanford.edu/data/glove.6B.zip'
    get_data(embedding_url, 'data/glove.6B.zip')
```

Phew, this might take a minute depending on your download speed. Once this is done, let's unzip the file, get it to the data directory, and convert it into `word2vec` format:

```
# !unzip data/glove.6B.zip
# !mv -v glove.6B.300d.txt data/glove.6B.300d.txt
# !mv -v glove.6B.200d.txt data/glove.6B.200d.txt
# !mv -v glove.6B.100d.txt data/glove.6B.100d.txt
# !mv -v glove.6B.50d.txt data/glove.6B.50d.txt

from gensim.scripts.glove2word2vec import glove2word2vec
glove_input_file = 'data/glove.6B.300d.txt'
word2vec_output_file = 'data/glove.6B.300d.txt.word2vec'
import os
if not os.path.exists(word2vec_output_file):
    glove2word2vec(glove_input_file, word2vec_output_file)
```

By the end of the preceding code block, we have the 300-dimension GloVe embedding from the official Stanford source converted into the word2vec format.

Let's load this into our working memory:

```
%%time
from gensim.models import KeyedVectors
filename = word2vec_output_file
embed = KeyedVectors.load_word2vec_format(word2vec_output_file,
binary=False)
```

Let's quickly check whether we can vectorize any word by checking for word embeddings for any word, for example, `awesome`:

```
assert embed['awesome'] is not None
```

`awesome`, this works!

Now, let's take a look at our first challenge.

Figuring out the right user intent

This is commonly referred to as the problem of intent categorization.

As a toy example, we will try to build an order bot that someone like DoorDash/Swiggy/Zomato might use.

Use case – food order bot

Consider the following sample sentence: *I'm looking for a cheap Chinese place in Indiranagar*.

We want to pick out Chinese as a cuisine type in the sentence. We can obviously take simple approaches, like exact substring matching (search *Chinese*) or TF-IDF-based matches.

Instead, we will generalize the model to discover cuisine types that we might not have identified yet, but that can learn about via the GloVe embedding.

We'll keep it as simple as possible: we'll provide some example cuisine types to tell the model that we need cuisines, and look for the most similar words in the sentence.

We'll loop through the words in the sentence and pick out the ones whose similarity to the reference words is above a certain threshold.

Do word vectors even work for this?

```
cuisine_refs = ["mexican", "thai", "british", "american", "italian"]
sample_sentence = "I'm looking for a cheap Indian or Chinese place in
Indiranagar"
```

For simplicity's sake, the following code is written as `for` loops, but can be vectorized for speed.

We iterate over each word in the input sentence and find the similarity score with respect to known cuisine words.

The higher the value, the more likely the word is to be something related to our cuisine references or `cuisine_refs`:

```
tokens = sample_sentence.split()
tokens = [x.lower().strip() for x in tokens]
threshold = 18.3
found = []
for term in tokens:
    if term in embed.vocab:
        scores = []
        for C in cuisine_refs:
            scores.append(np.dot(embed[C], embed[term].T))
            # hint replace above above np.dot with:
            # scores.append(embed.cosine_similarities(<vector1>,
<vector_all_others>))
        mean_score = np.mean(scores)
        print(f"{term}: {mean_score}")
        if mean_score > threshold:
            found.append(term)
print(found)
```

The following is the corresponding output:

```
looking: 7.448504447937012
for: 10.627421379089355
a: 11.809560775756836
cheap: 7.09670877456665
indian: 18.64516258239746
or: 9.692893981933594
chinese: 19.09498405456543
place: 7.651237487792969
in: 10.085711479187012
['indian', 'chinese']
```

The threshold is determined empirically. Notice that we are able to infer *Indian* and *Chinese* as cuisines, even if they are not part of the original set.

Of course, exact matches will have a much higher score.

This is a good example where there's a better problem formulation in terms of the *generic* cuisine type that can be learned. This is more helpful than a dictionary-based cuisine type. This also proves that we can rely on word-vector-based approaches.

Can we extend this for user intent classification? Let's try this next.

Classifying user intent

We want to be able to put sentences into categories by user *intents*. Intents are a generic mechanism that combine multiple individual examples into one semantic umbrella. For example, *hi, hey, good morning*, and *wassup!* are all examples of the _greeting_ intent.

Using *greeting* as an input, the backend logic can then determine how to respond to the user.

There are many ways we could combine word vectors to represent a sentence, but again we're going to do the simplest thing possible: add them up.

This is definitely a less-than-ideal solution, but works in practice because of the simple, unsupervised approach we use with this:

```
def sum_vecs(embed,text):

    tokens = text.split(' ')
    vec = np.zeros(embed.vector_size)

    for idx, term in enumerate(tokens):
        if term in embed.vocab:
            vec = vec + embed[term]
    return vec

sentence_vector = sum_vecs(embed, sample_sentence)
print(sentence_vector.shape)
>> (300,)
```

Let's define a data dictionary with some examples for each intent.

We will be using the data dictionary written by `Alan at the Rasa Blog` for this.

This dictionary can be updated since we have more user input:

```
data={
  "greet": {
    "examples" : ["hello","hey you","howdy","hello","hi","hey there","hey ho", "ssup?"],
    "centroid" : None
  },
  "inform": {
    "examples" : [
        "i'd like something asian",
        "maybe korean",
        "what swedish options do i have",
        "what italian options do i have",
        "i want korean food",
        "i want vegetarian food",
        "i would like chinese food",
        "what japanese options do i have",
        "vietnamese please",
        "i want some chicken",
        "maybe thai",
        "i'd like something vegetarian",
        "show me British restaurants",
        "show me a cool malay spot",
        "where can I get some spicy food"
    ],
    "centroid" : None
  },
  "deny": {
    "examples" : [
      "no thanks"
      "any other places ?",
      "something else",
      "naah",
      "not that one",
      "i do not like that",
      "something else",
      "please nooo"
      "show other options?"
    ],
    "centroid" : None
  },
    "affirm":{
        "examples":[
            "yeah",
            "that works",
            "good, thanks",
            "this works",
```

```
                "sounds good",
                "thanks, this is perfect",
                "just what I wanted"
            ],
            "centroid": None
        }

    }
```

The approach we have is simple: we find the centroid of each *user intent*. A centroid is just a central point to denote each intent. Then, the incoming text is assigned to the user intent that's nearest to the corresponding cluster.

Let's write a simple function to find the centroid and update the dictionary:

```
    def get_centroid(embed,examples):
        C = np.zeros((len(examples),embed.vector_size))
        for idx, text in enumerate(examples):
            C[idx,:] = sum_vecs(embed,text)

        centroid = np.mean(C,axis=0)
        assert centroid.shape[0] == embed.vector_size
        return centroid
```

Let's add the centroid to the data dictionary:

```
    for label in data.keys():
        data[label]["centroid"] = get_centroid(embed,data[label]["examples"])
```

Let's write a simple function to find the nearest user intent cluster now. We will use the L2 norm that we already implemented in `np.linalg`:

```
    def get_intent(embed,data, text):
        intents = list(data.keys())
        vec = sum_vecs(embed,text)
        scores = np.array([ np.linalg.norm(vec-data[label]["centroid"]) for label in intents])
        return intents[np.argmin(scores)]
```

Let's run this on some user text that is **not** in the **data dictionary**:

```
    for text in ["hey ","i am looking for chinese food","not for me", "ok, this is good"]:
        print(f"text : '{text}', predicted_label : '{get_intent(embed, data, text)}'")
```

The corresponding code generalizes well, and is convincing regarding the fact that this is good enough for the roughly 10-15 minutes it took for us to get to this point:

```
text : 'hey ', predicted_label : 'greet'
text : 'i am looking for chinese food', predicted_label : 'inform'
text : 'not for me', predicted_label : 'deny'
text : 'ok, this is good', predicted_label : 'affirm'
```

Bot responses

We now know how to understand and categorize user intent. We now need to simply respond to each user intent with some corresponding responses. Let's get these *template* bot responses in one place:

```
templates = {
        "utter_greet": ["hey there!", "Hey! How you doin'? "],
        "utter_options": ["ok, let me check some more"],
        "utter_goodbye": ["Great, I'll go now. Bye bye", "bye bye", "Goodbye!"],
        "utter_default": ["Sorry, I didn't quite follow"],
        "utter_confirm": ["Got it", "Gotcha", "Your order is confirmed now"]
    }
```

Storing the `Response` map in a separate entity is helpful. This means that you can generate responses at a separate service from your intent understanding module and then glue them together:

```
response_map = {
    "greet": "utter_greet",
    "affirm": "utter_goodbye",
    "deny": "utter_options",
    "inform": "utter_confirm",
    "default": "utter_default",
}
```

If we think about this a little bit more, there is no need for the response map to be depend only on the intent that's categorized. You can convert this response map into a separate function that generates the map using related context and then picks a bot template.

But here, for simplicity, let's keep it as a dictionary/JSON-style structure.

Let's write a simple `get_bot_response` function that takes in the response mapping, templates, and the intent as input and returns the actual bot response:

```
import random
def get_bot_response(bot_response_map, bot_templates, intent):
    if intent not in list(response_map):
        intent = "default"
    select_template = bot_response_map[intent]
    templates = bot_templates[select_template]
    return random.choice(templates)
```

Let's quickly try this with one sentence:

```
user_intent = get_intent(embed, data, "i want indian food")
get_bot_response(response_map, templates, user_intent)
```

The code is free of syntax errors at this point. This seems good to go for more performance testing. But before that, how can we make this better?

Better response personalization

You'll notice that the function picks one template at random for any particular *bot intent*, so to say. While this is for simplicity here, in practice, you can train an ML model to pick a response that's personalized to a user.

A simple personalization to make is to adapt with the talking/typing of the user's style. For example, one user might be formal with, *Hello, how are you today?*, while another might be more informal with, *Yo*.

Therefore, *Hello* gets *Goodbye!* in response while *Yo!* gets *Bye bye* or even *TTYL* in the same conversation.

For now, let's go ahead and check the bot response for the sentences that we have already seen:

```
for text in ["hey","i am looking for italian food","not for me", "ok, this is good"]:
    user_intent = get_intent(embed, data, text)
    bot_reply = get_bot_response(response_map, templates, user_intent)
    print(f"text : '{text}', intent: {user_intent}, bot: {bot_reply}")
```

The responses can vary due to randomness; here is an example:

```
text : 'hey', intent: greet, bot: Hey! How you doin'?
text : 'i am looking for italian food', intent: inform, bot: Gotcha
text : 'not for me', intent: deny, bot: ok, let me check some more
text : 'ok, this is good', intent: affirm, bot: Goodbye!
```

Summary

In this chapter on chatbots, we learned about *intent*, which usually refers to the user input, *response*, which is via the bot, *templates*, which defines the nature of bot responses, and *entities*, such as cuisine type, in our example.

Additionally, to understand the user intent—and even find entities—we used **unsupervised approaches**, that is, we did not have training examples this time. In practice, most commercial systems use a hybrid system, combining supervised and unsupervised systems.

The one thing you should take away from here is that we don't need a lot of training data to make the first usable version of a bot for a specific use case.

8
Web Deployments

So far, we have been focused on getting something to work for the very first time and then making incremental updates. These updates are almost always geared toward better techniques and better usability. But, how do we expose them to the user? One way to do this is via REST endpoints.

In this chapter, we are going to cover the following topics:

- Training a model, and writing some neater utils for data I/O
- Building a predict function, separated from training
- Exposing what we have covered using a Flask REST endpoint

Web deployments

This is the hackathon version, and more experienced engineers will notice that we neglect a lot of best practices in favor of saving developer time. In my defense, I did add pretty usable logging.

We will start from where we left off when we talked about text classification using machine learning methods. There are a few challenges that we left untouched:

- **Model persistence**: How can I write the model, data, and code to disk?
- **Model loading and prediction**: How can I load the model data *and code* from disk?
- **Flask for REST endpoints**: How can I expose the loaded model over the web?

If there is anything that you take away from this chapter, it should be the preceding three questions. If you have a clear and complete idea regarding how to tackle these three questions, your battle is won.

We will use a scikit-learn model and the same TF-IDF based pipelines we are familiar with for this demo.

Model persistence

The first challenge is to write the model data and code it to disk. Let's start by training the pipeline first.

Let's get the imports out of the way:

```
import gzip
import logging
import os
from pathlib import Path
from urllib.request import urlretrieve
import numpy as np
import pandas as pd
from sklearn.externals import joblib
from sklearn.feature_extraction.text import CountVectorizer, TfidfTransformer
from sklearn.linear_model import LogisticRegression as LR
from sklearn.pipeline import Pipeline
from tqdm import tqdm
```

Let's write some utils for reading the data from text files and downloading them if absent:

Let's start by setting up a download progress bar for our use. We will do this by building a small abstraction over the `tqdm` package:

```
class TqdmUpTo(tqdm):
    def update_to(self, b=1, bsize=1, tsize=None):
        if tsize is not None:
        self.total = tsize
        self.update(b * bsize - self.n)
```

Let's use the preceding `tqdm` progress information for defining a download utility:

```
def get_data(url, filename):
    """
    Download data if the filename does not exist already
    Uses Tqdm to show download progress
    """
    if not os.path.exists(filename):
        dirname = os.path.dirname(filename)
        if not os.path.exists(dirname):
            os.makedirs(dirname)
        with TqdmUpTo(unit="B", unit_scale=True, miniters=1, desc=url.split("/")[-1]) as t:
            urlretrieve(url, filename, reporthook=t.update_to)
```

Notice that the utility uses os instead of pathlib, which is preferred throughout the text otherwise. This is both for variety and the fact that os works equally well in Python 2, while pathlib is best used with Python 3.4 or later. As a reminder, this entire book assumes that you are using Python 3.6 code.

Now that we have a get_data utility in place, let's write a read_data utility, which is customized to our specific dataset:

```python
def read_data(dir_path):
    """read data into pandas dataframe"""
    def load_dir_reviews(reviews_path):
        files_list = list(reviews_path.iterdir())
        reviews = []
        for filename in files_list:
        f = open(filename, "r", encoding="utf-8")
        reviews.append(f.read())
        return pd.DataFrame({"text": reviews})
    pos_path = dir_path / "pos"
    neg_path = dir_path / "neg"
    pos_reviews, neg_reviews = load_dir_reviews(pos_path), load_dir_reviews(neg_path)
    pos_reviews["label"] = 1
    neg_reviews["label"] = 0
    merged = pd.concat([pos_reviews, neg_reviews])
    df = merged.sample(frac=1.0) # shuffle the rows
    df.reset_index(inplace=True) # don't carry index from previous
    df.drop(columns=["index"], inplace=True) # drop the column 'index'
    return df
```

pandas DataFrames make our code much easier to read, manage, and debug. Additionally, this function actually uses a Python nested function to make it easier to increase code reuse. Notice that for both positive and negative reviews, we use the same internal function that does the I/O for us.

Let's import these utils now:

```
from utils import get_data, read_data
```

I have defined a logger from the Python 3 logging module, with both the file handler and the console handler. Since that is a well-known and established best practice, I am going to skip that here and use the logger directly instead:

```
data_path = Path(os.getcwd()) / "data" / "aclImdb"
logger.info(data_path)
```

The `data_path` variable now contains the extracted folders and files from `aclImdb`. Notice that this extraction is not done by code, but is instead done by the user outside of this code.

This is because this extraction from `*.tar.gz` or `*.tgz` is OS-dependent. Another thing that you should have noticed by now is that we have moved away from notebooks with interspersed print statements and previews to Python scripts for this section.

We must download the compressed file – which is a little more than 110 MB – if it does not exist in the target location:

```
if not data_path.exists():
    data_url = "http://files.fast.ai/data/aclImdb.tgz"
    get_data(data_url, "data/imdb.tgz")
```

Extract the files while you're offline before trying to read them:

```
train_path = data_path / "train"
# load data file as dict object
train = read_data(train_path)
```

The `train` variable is now a DataFrame with two columns: the raw *text* and the *label*. The label is either `pos` or `neg`, which is short for positive or negative. The label indicates the overall sentiment of the review. We separate these into two variables: `X_train` and `y_train`:

```
# extract the images (X) and labels (y) from the dict
X_train, y_train = train["text"], train["label"]
```

Next, let's define the `Pipeline` of operations that we want to perform. The logistic regression model, which uses TF-IDF representations, is the simplest and fastest way to train the model, and has reasonably good performance. We will use that here, but you can (*and usually, should*) actually replace this with whatever has the best performance on your test data:

```
lr_clf = Pipeline(
 [("vect", CountVectorizer()), ("tfidf", TfidfTransformer()), ("clf",
LR())]
)
lr_clf.fit(X=X_train, y=y_train)
```

Once we call the `.fit` function, we have trained our pipeline for text classification.

Those who are familiar with Python might remember pickle or cPickle. Pickle is a Python-native utility for saving objects and other Python data structures to disk in binary for later reuse. `joblib` is a pickle improvement!

joblib is an improvement because it also caches the *code with data*, which is fantastic for our use case. We don't have to worry about defining the pipeline in our web API layer. It is no longer tied to our specific model, which means that we can keep making better releases by simply changing the underlying joblib.dump file.

As a tribute to the classic Python pickle, we are going to give a .pkl extension to this cached code and model.pkl data file:

```
# save model
joblib.dump(lr_clf, "model.pkl")
```

That's it! We have now written our code and data logic into one single binary file.

How will we actually use this? Let's look at how next.

Model loading and prediction

The next challenge is actually to load the model from our pickled file and use it to make predictions.

Let's start by loading the model from disk:

```
from sklearn.externals import joblib
model = joblib.load("model.pkl")
```

The model variable should now expose all the functions that the original lr_clf object did. Of all those methods, we are interested in the predict function.

But before we use that, let's load some files from disk for making predictions:

```
# loading one example negative review
with open(r".\\data\\aclImdb\\train\neg\\1_1.txt", "r") as infile:
    test_neg_contents = infile.read()

# loading one example positive review
with open(r".\\data\\aclImdb\\train\pos\\0_9.txt", "r") as infile:
    test_pos_contents = infile.read()
```

We can now pass these variables in a list to the predict method:

```
predictions = model.predict([test_neg_contents, test_pos_contents])
```

What does the predictions variable contain at this point?

Is it a list? Is it a numpy array? Or just an integer?

You can check for this by using the following code:

```
print(predictions)
> [0 1]

for p in predictions:
    print("pos" if p else "neg")

> neg
> pos
```

As we can see, the predictions is a list of integers, identical to the way we had read our `y_train` variable in the training file. Let's go ahead and incorporate what we have learned here into a web interface and REST Endpoints.

Flask for web deployments

Let's begin by getting the imports out of the way:

```
import logging
import flask
import os
import numpy as np
from flask import Flask, jsonify, render_template, request
from sklearn.externals import joblib
```

I am assuming that as a programmer, you can pick up Flask basics outside this book. Even then, for the sake of completeness, I am adding the main ideas that are relevant to us:

- The main web app is defined in the `Flask` module, which is imported from Flask
- `jsonify` converts any JSON-friendly dictionary into a JSON that can then be returned to the user
- `render_template` is how we expose HTML pages and web interfaces to our users

Let's begin by declaring our app first:

```
app = Flask(__name__)
```

Next, we will use the `route` function to decorate our Python functions and expose them as REST endpoints. Let's start by exposing a simple status endpoint that is always ON and return 200 for whenever the service is running:

```
@app.route("/status", methods=["GET"])
def get_status():
    return jsonify({"version": "0.0.1", "status": True})
```

The `methods` variable is usually a list of strings with the values GET POST, or both. GET is used for HTTP(S) GET calls that require no information from the user, except that which is already contained in the GET call. The HTTP POST calls supply additional data from the client (such as the browser) to the server.

This can be accessed by hitting the `/status` endpoint in your browser.

Go ahead and try it.

Ouch! We forgot to run the app itself first.

Let's go ahead and run the app in debug mode. Debug mode allows us to add and edit code, and automatically load the code on every save:

```
if __name__ == "__main__":
    # load ml model from disk
    model = joblib.load("model.pkl")
    # start api
    app.run(host="0.0.0.0", port=8000, debug=True)
```

Notice that we load the `model` variable from `joblib`, like we did earlier. This code segment is written at the end of an `api.py` file. This is remarkably sloppy, with no concurrency support, and isn't integrated with nginx – but all of that is fine for this demonstration.

What happens if we hit the `localhost:8000/status` endpoint from our browser now?

We get a status 200, and the data field contains our JSON with the version and *status* information. Great.

Web Deployments

Let's go ahead and add our `/predict` endpoint. Here is the outline of the steps this function will undertake:

1. It will check if this is indeed a POST method. If yes, it will extract the file information from the *file* key in `flask.request.files`.
2. Then, it will write this file to disk and read again, and then pass string text to `model.predict` as a single element of a list.
3. Finally, it will return the result to a web interface in HTML, after optionally deleting the file written to disk:

```python
@app.route("/predict", methods=["POST"])
def make_prediction():
    if request.method == "POST":
        # get uploaded file if it exists
        logger.debug(request.files)
        f = request.files["file"]
        f.save(f.filename) # save file to disk
        logger.info(f"{f.filename} saved to disk")
        # read file from disk
        with open(f.filename, "r") as infile:
            text_content = infile.read()
            logger.info(f"Text Content from file read")
        prediction = model.predict([text_content])
        logger.info(f"prediction: {prediction}")
        prediction = "pos" if prediction[0] == 1 else "neg"
        os.remove(f.filename)
    return flask.render_template("index.html", label=prediction)
```

Quite obviously, the step for writing the file to disk is redundant if we are simply going to delete it later. In practice, I keep the files on disk since it helps with debugging and, in some cases, understanding how the API is being used in actual practice by its users.

In the preceding snippet, you might have noticed that we return an `index.html` file with a `label` value. The label is set as part of `Jinja2` templates. The variable is used in the `index.html` itself and the value is updated when rendering the page.

This is the `index.html` we will use:

```html
<html>
<head>
<title>Text Classification model as a Flask API</title>
<meta charset="utf-8">
<meta name="viewport" content="width=device-width, initial-scale=1">
</head>
```

```
<body>
<h1>Movie Sentiment Analysis</h1>
<form action="/predict" method="post" enctype="multipart/form-data">
 <input type="file" name="file" value="Upload">
 <input type="submit" value="Predict">
 <p>Prediction: {% if label %} {{ label }} {% endif %}</p>
</form>
</body>
</html>
```

This is what the HTML looks like:

The **Prediction: pos** is actually a result from the file I uploaded to this page earlier. This was marked by the {%%} syntax in the actual HTML:

```
Prediction: {% if label %} {{ label }} {% endif %}
```

So, we have seen a few things in the Flask-based web deployment section:

- How do you receive uploaded files on the Flask webserver?
- How do you upload the file using a web interface?
- And, as a bonus: Jinja templates to display the returned answer

 It is worth mentioning that we could make this even more general by separating returns. This would be for use by humans, where we return HTML, and for use by machine, where we return JSON. I leave this function refactoring as an exercise for you.

Quite obviously, we could have done this with Django or any other web framework. The only reason I picked Flask is for demonstration purposes and because it is very lightweight, with no concern for model-view-controller separation.

Summary

The key takeaway from this chapter should be that any machine learning model can be deployed like any other piece of code. The only difference is that we have to make room for being able to load the model again from disk. To do this, first, we need to train a model and write the model code and weights to disk using `joblib`. Then, we need to build a predict function, which is separated from training. Finally, we expose what we have done by using Flash with Jinja2 HTML templates.

Other Books You May Enjoy

If you enjoyed this book, you may be interested in these other books by Packt:

Natural Language Processing with Java

Richard M Reese

ISBN: 978-1-78439-179-9

- Develop a deep understanding of the basic NLP tasks and how they relate to each other
- Discover and use the available tokenization engines
- Implement techniques for end of sentence detection
- Apply search techniques to find people and things within a document
- Construct solutions to identify parts of speech within sentences
- Use parsers to extract relationships between elements of a document
- Integrate basic tasks to tackle more complex NLP problems

Mastering Natural Language Processing with Python

Deepti Chopra, Nisheeth Joshi, Et al

ISBN:978-1-78398-904-1

- Implement string matching algorithms and normalization techniques
- Implement statistical language modeling techniques
- Get an insight into developing a stemmer, lemmatizer, morphological analyzer, and morphological generator
- Develop a search engine and implement POS tagging concepts and statistical modeling concepts involving the n gram approach
- Familiarize yourself with concepts such as the Treebank construct, CFG construction, the CYK Chart Parsing algorithm, and the Earley Chart Parsing algorithm
- Develop an NER-based system and understand and apply the concepts of sentiment analysis
- Understand and implement the concepts of Information Retrieval and text summarization
- Develop a Discourse Analysis System and Anaphora Resolution based system

Leave a review - let other readers know what you think

Please share your thoughts on this book with others by leaving a review on the site that you bought it from. If you purchased the book from Amazon, please leave us an honest review on this book's Amazon page. This is vital so that other potential readers can see and use your unbiased opinion to make purchasing decisions, we can understand what our customers think about our products, and our authors can see your feedback on the title that they have worked with Packt to create. It will only take a few minutes of your time, but is valuable to other potential customers, our authors, and Packt. Thank you!

Index

A
automatic question generation
   about 57
   part-of-speech tagging 57, 58
   ruleset, creating 59, 60

B
BatchWrapper 131

C
chatbots
   about 141
   building 142
   response personalization 150, 151
   responses 149, 150
   using, as learning example 141
CoreNLP
   versus spaCy 36
corpus
   cleaning, with FlashText 44, 47
correlated classifiers
   removing 110, 111

D
data exploration 88, 89
data loaders 123
dataset
   vectorizing 70, 72
decision trees 101
deep learning
   about 114, 115
   puzzle pieces 115
   training loop 117
dependency parsing
   used, for question and answer generation 61, 62
doc2vec API
   about 84
   hierarchical softmax 85, 87
   negative sampling 85
document embedding 81, 83

E
ensemble models
   about 107
   correlated classifiers, removing 110, 111
   voting ensembles 107, 108, 109
   weighted classifiers 109
extra trees classifier 102

F
fastText embedddings
   fastText, versus word2vec 81
   training 79, 80
   word2vec embeddings, training 80
FlashText
   used, for cleaning corpus 44, 47
FuzzyWuzzy
   used, for spelling errors correction 37, 39

G
General Data Processing Regulation (GDPR) 51
GridSearch
   executing, on LogisticRegression parameter 106, 107

H
hack, tokenization
   regexes 27, 29
heuristics 142, 144
hierarchical softmax 85, 87

I

iterators, text categorization
   BucketIterator 129, 131

J

Jellyfish
   used, for spelling errors correction 39, 41

K

Kaggle API
   used, for obtaining data 118
KeyedVectors API
   used, for word representations 74, 76

L

lemmatization, with spaCy
   -PRON- 36
   case-insensitive 36
   conversion 36
lemmatization
   about 34
   with spaCy 34
linguistics 49, 50
logistic regression
   about 93, 97
   ngram range, increasing 99
   stop words, removing 98

M

machine learning
   for text 92, 93
model evaluation 88, 89
modern machine learning methods
   comparing 114
Multinomial Naive Bayes
   about 99
   fit prior, changing to false 100
   stop words, removing 99
   TF-IDF, adding 99

N

named entity recognition
   used, for redacting names 51, 53
   with question and answer generation 68
Natural Language Processing (NLP)
   about 6, 21, 49, 50
   need for 6, 7, 8
   workflow template 8
Natural Language Toolkit (NLTK)
   versus spaCy 36
negative sampling 85

O

Out of Vocabulary (OOV)
   about 76
   dataset, obtaining 77, 78
   handling 77

P

Pandas
   data, reading into 95
parameter tuning
   with RandomizedSearch 103, 105
phonetic encoding 40, 42, 44
phonetic word similarity
   runtime complexity 44
   used, for spelling errors correction 41
pre-trained embeddings
   using 73
puzzling factors, deep learning
   loss function 116
   model 116
   optimizer 117
PyTorch
   need for 121

Q

question and answer generation
   leveling up 66, 68
   with dependency parsing 61, 62

R

random forest classifier 102
RandomizedSearch
   used, for parameter tuning 103, 105
recurrent neural networks (RNN) 113
regexes 27, 29

right user intent
  classifying 146, 148, 149
  figuring 144
  use case 144, 145

S

sentence tokenization 31
sentiment analysis, as text classification
  ensemble methods 93
  simple classifiers 93
  simple classifiers, optimizing 93
sentiment analysis
  using, as text classification 93
simple classifiers
  about 93, 96
  decision trees 101
  Multinomial Naive Bayes 99
  optimizing 103
  support vector machines 100
spaCy tokenizer
  working 30
spaCy
  entity types 55, 56
  installing 50
  relationship, visualizing 62, 64
  tasks 22
  textacy 51
  used, for lemmatization 34
  used, for tokenization 29
  versus CoreNLP 36
  versus NLTK 36
spelling errors correction
  phonetic word similarity 41
  with FuzzyWuzzy 37, 39
  with Jellyfish 39, 41
spelling errors
  correcting 37
stemming 34
support vector machines 100

T

tasks, spaCy
  data, loading 22, 24
  loaded data, exploring 25
text categorization

about 118
BatchWrapper 131
challenge 118
data loaders 123
data, exploring 119, 120
data, obtaining with Kaggle API 118
dataset objects, exploring 126, 128
field class, exploring 124, 126
iterators 129
multiple target dataset 120
naming conventions 123
PyTorch, installing 122
PyTorch, need for 121
style 123
torchtext 123
torchtext, installing 122
text classification workflow
  about 12
  data, obtaining 13
  environment setup 12, 13
  ML algorithm, executing with sklearn 15, 17, 19
  numbers, assigning to text 14, 15
text classifier model
  initializing 134, 135
  loss function 135
  optimizer 135
  prediction mode 138
  predictions, converting into pandas DataFrame 138
  training 133
  training loop 136, 138
textacy 51, 64, 65
tokenization
  about 26
  case change 31, 34
  hack 27
  intuitive 26
  stop words removal 31, 34
  with spaCy 29
torchtext 123

U

urlretrieve
  used, for obtaining data 94, 95

V

voting ensembles
  hard voting 107, 108
  soft voting 109

W

web deployments
  about 153
  flask 158, 160, 161
  model persistence 154, 156, 157
  model, loading 157
  prediction 157
weighted classifiers 109
word representations
  about 72
  fastText embedddings, training 79, 80
  pre-trained embeddings, using 73
  with KeyedVectors API 74, 76
word vectors 142, 144
word2vec embeddings
  training 80
word2vec
  versus fastText 81
workflow template, NLP
  algorithms, improving 10
  algorithms, iterating 10
  data 9
  data, preparing 9
  deployment 11
  evaluation 11
  problem 9
  quick wins 9

www.ingramcontent.com/pod-product-compliance
Lightning Source LLC
Chambersburg PA
CBHW082247220526
45469CB00009B/2903